Frank Hamilton Taylor, Exchange Philadelphia Maritime

The Hand Book of the lower Delaware River

Ports, Tides, Pilots, Quarantine Stations, Light House Service, Life Saving and

Maritime Reporting Stations

Frank Hamilton Taylor, Exchange Philadelphia Maritime

The Hand Book of the lower Delaware River
Ports, Tides, Pilots, Quarantine Stations, Light House Service, Life Saving and Maritime Reporting Stations

ISBN/EAN: 9783337250201

Printed in Europe, USA, Canada, Australia, Japan

Cover: Foto ©Andreas Hilbeck / pixelio.de

More available books at **www.hansebooks.com**

GEO. V. CRESSON CO.
POWER TRANSMITTING MACHINERY

MAIN OFFICE AND WORKS, 18th STREET and ALLEGHENY AVENUE, PHILADA., PA.

NEW YORK OFFICE, 136 LIBERTY STREET.

FOUNDED A. D. 1818

PHILADELPHIA　　　　　　　　　　　　NEW YORK

JACOB G. NEAFIE　　　　MATHIAS SEDDINGER　　　　CHAS. HALYBURTON
President　　　　　　　Vice-President　　　　　　Sec'y and Treas.

ESTABLISHED 1838

The Neafie & Levy Ship and Engine Building Company

Penn Works

Iron and Steel Ship and Engine Builders of every Description

Beach and Palmer Streets

Steamship Repairs a Specialty　　　　　　　　PHILADELPHIA

INDEX OF CHAPTERS.

	PAGE
Launch of the S. S. St. Louis	3
The Delaware River—From Source to the Sea	5
First Exploration	5
Dutch and Swedish Colonists	6
First Organized Government	8
Capture of Fort Christina	8
The Holland Patent, Old Swedish Churches	8
Philadelphia Planned	9
Penn's Treaty	11
Philadelphia the National Capital, A great Industrial Metropolis, Birthplace of Steam Navigation	13
Historic Landmarks, Battle of Red Bank, Siege of Fort Mifflin	18
Philadelphia's Water Front	15
Advantages for Manufacturers	17
Removal of the Islands, New Railroad Bridge, State Quarantine Station	18
National Quarantine	23
Breakwater Station	24
Reedy Island Station	29
The Philadelphia Maritime Exchange	37
Reporting Stations	59
Life-Saving Service	62
Pilot Boats, City Ice Boats	67
Lights of the Delaware	69
Ship Building	73
Delaware River Defences, The Great Navy Yard of the Future	77
Removal of Obstructions below Philadelphia	81
Harbor and River Improvment, Delaware Avenue Improvement	83
Chester, Wilmington and other Ports	85
School Ship Saratoga	87
Naval Reserves, Distances	89
Value of Exports and Imports	89
Commerce of the Port of Philadelphia for Ten Years	90
Arrivals at Delaware Breakwater in 1894, Coast Line Distances	91
Survey Charts of the Delaware Bay and River, Shipping Terms, Nautical Measures	92
Directory of Commercial and Maritime Associations in Philadelphia, Public Offices	93
Foreign Consuls	94
New Offices, Directors and Committees of the Philadelphia Maritime Exchange	96

Carstairs' Monogram Rye Whiskey

Carstairs, McCall & Co.

222 S. Front St.   1 State Street
PHILADELPHIA   NEW YORK

◉ WING to a steadily increasing demand from private parties for our well known brand of Whiskey

"CARSTAIRS' MONOGRAM"

We are now putting it up in cases, and request you will give it a trial.

We guarantee these goods to be the oldest and finest Rye Whiskey cased. Price, $18.00 per case of 12 bottles each.

For sale by the following well known houses:

E. J. CRIPPEN & CO.   SHOWELL & FRYER
MITCHELL, FLETCHER & CO.   LELAR & COMPANY

LIST OF ADVERTISERS

	PAGE
American Dredging Co.	27
Atlantic Refining Company, The	12
Baizley, John	19
Baldwin Locomotive Works	30
Barney & Co., Charles D.	4
Bartram, The	35
Berwind-White Coal Mining Co	30
Branson Machine Co.	17
Brill Company, J. G.	43
British and Foreign Marine Insurance Co., Ltd.	41
Brockie & Welsh	5
Brown Brothers & Co.	41
Carnahan & Ennis	39
Carstairs, McCall & Co.	c
Chandler & Co., Alfred N.	8
Chapman Derrick and Wrecking Co.	48
Clyde Steamship Co., The	24
Cramp's Ship Yard	Second Page of Cover
Cresson Co., Geo. V.	a
Crew, Levick & Co.	47
Delaware Insurance Co., The	29
Earn Line Steamship Company, The	11
Electro Phototype Co., The	17
Evans, Louis P.	32
Fall River Line	20
Felton, Sibley & Co	21
Flanagan, S. & Jas. M.	42
Franklin Sugar Refining Co., The	25
Garrett & Sons, W. E	32
Gas Engine and Power Co.	48
Gillingham, Garrison & Co., Limited	39
Girard Point Storage Company	44
Godley's Storage Warehouses	33
Graham-Meyer Torch and Liquid Light Co., Inc.	22
Guarantors Liability Indemnity Company of Pennsylvania, The	16
Hagan & Co., Peter	5
Hagar & Co., W. F.	40
Hale & Kilburn Mfg. Co., The	46
Halyburton, Jr., C	39
Hampton, Jr., & Co., J. W	21
Hannis Distilling Co., The	39
Harlan & Hollingsworth Company, The	19
Hempstead & Son, O. G	20
Hibbs, E. A.	21
Hillman Ship and Eng. Bldg. Co., The Chas.	2
Hoopes & Townsend	18
Horstmann Company, Wm. H.	8
Insurance Company of North America	14-15
International Navigation Company	13
Janney & Co., O. S.	46

	PAGE
Johnson & Higgins	21
Keen, Sutterle Co.	37
Kensington Engine Works, Limited	3
Keystone Detective Agency	39
Lesley & Trinkle	32
Levis & Co., Henry	14
Maritime Exchange Reporting Station, The	34
Mather & Co.	45
McCahan Sugar Refining Co., The W. J.	26
McDonough & Co., M. F.	29
Moore & Sinnott	31
Moore & Sons Co., Enoch	29
Morris, Tasker & Co. (Inc.)	10
Morse, Williams & Co.	46
Neafie & Levy Ship and Eng. Bldg. Co., The	b
Newhall Engineering Co. Geo. M., Limited	23
Newport News Ship Bldg. and Dry Dock Co.	6
Pain's Fireworks Co.	40
Palace Steamer Republic	9
Parr & Son, I. M., Limited	17
Pennsylvania Railroad Co.	Third Page of Cover
Penna. Warehousing and Safe Deposit Co.	7
Philadelphia Engineering Works, Limited	4
Philadelphia Grain Elevator Co., The	9
Philadelphia Shipping Company	6
Plumb, Fayette R.	22
Powers & Weightman	b
Pusey & Jones Co., The	33
Quaker City Cooperage Co.	20
Red Star Tugs	28
Robert Hare Powel Co.	39
Samuel, Frank	45
Scott, George W	8
Seaboard Oil Works	44
Segal, A	46
Sellers & Co., Wm. (Inc.)	1
Sheppard & Co., Isaac A.	28
Shinn & Co	42
Smithers & Co., W. H	23
Southwark Foundry and Machine Co.	7
Spreckels Sugar Refining Company	3
Sterling Coal Co.	2
Stetson Co., John B	4
Strawbridge & Clothier	5
Taylor's Sons, Chas. M.	9
Upper Delaware River Transportation Co.	36
Wetherill Company, The S. P.	19
White Dental Mfg. Co., The S. S.	d
Williamson & Cassedy	40
Wilmington & Northern R. R.	38

The S. S. White Dental Mfg. Co.

Chestnut Street, Cor. Twelfth, Philadelphia

BRANCHES:

New York   Boston   Chicago   Brooklyn   Atlanta

Manufacturers of every article used by the Dental Profession, either in the office or laboratory.

Established in 1844, this house has rounded out its full half century of successful progress without a check, and without vanity it can claim the application of this quotation:

"Leadership means superiority. Continued leadership implies progress. Tacitly acknowledged leadership over many competitors shows undeniable merit. Enduring success must be founded on intrinsic worth. Reputation does not long survive the qualities upon which it was founded."

THE HAND BOOK

OF THE

Lower Delaware River

PORTS, TIDES, PILOTS, QUARANTINE STATIONS,
LIGHT-HOUSE SERVICE, LIFE-SAVING AND MARITIME REPORTING STATIONS

ISSUED UNDER DIRECTION OF

THE PHILADELPHIA MARITIME EXCHANGE

PREPARED AND ILLUSTRATED BY

FRANK H. TAYLOR

GEO. S. HARRIS & SONS, PRINTERS
718 ARCH STREET, PHILADA.
1895

COPYRIGHT, 1898
BY THE PHILADELPHIA MARITIME EXCHANGE

LAUNCH OF THE S.S. ST. LOUIS, AT THE CRAMP SHIP YARDS, PHILADELPHIA, NOVEMBER 12, 1894—THE LARGEST AMERICAN SHIP.

[Illustration, by permission, from "Once a Week."]

The Delaware River.

From Source to the Sea.

THE sources of the Delaware River are found under the western shadows of the Catskill Mountains in the State of New York. Its east and west branches, flowing thence upon either side of a lateral range of highlands, are united near Port Deposit, and upon its course to the sea the stream forms the partial boundary line of four populous States. The upper reaches of the Delaware for two hundred or more miles present a continuous series of beautiful vistas much loved by the landscape artist and favored by the angler, where long and placid intervals between lofty promontories are broken by swift rapids as the river gathers volume on its way. Its principal tributary is the equally picturesque Lehigh River, meeting it at Easton, and the outflow below this point drains a territory of 11,000 square miles. The Delaware River first lends itself to the uses of navigation at Trenton, N. J., to which point river steamers regularly ply, the depth of the channel varying from seven feet near Bordentown to thirty-nine feet at the mouth of Frankford Creek. In front of Philadelphia, and from this city to the sea, a distance of 103 miles, the depth is sufficient for the largest sea going ships at the load line. From the last of its rapid shallows the bed of the river is that of an alluvial tidal estuary, broadened by the erosion of ages and flowing with the influx and retreat of each day's tides between shores fringed with groves, bordered by broad farms, embellished by splendid country seats and emphasized by vast and infinitely varied industries. It is one of the great marine highways of the world.

THE UPPER DELAWARE

First Exploration—1611.

When Thomas West, Lord de la Ware, was sailing southward in 1611 along the mysterious coast of New Jersey upon his way to assume the duties of Governor of the young colony of Virginia, then four years old, he was driven by stress of weather into the wide water between the capes at the jaws of the river, and ascending it cautiously with lead line, he found upon the site of Philadelphia the Indian Settlement of Coquannock, "the grove of long pine trees," a capital town of the aggressive nation called the Lenni Lenapes, and whose great chief was Tamanend, whence the present name of "Tammany."

There were several names for the river in the Indian nomenclature of the region. The people of the capital town called it the "Lenape Wihituck."

When a Swedish expedition came, the Bay Indians told them it was called the "Pantoxet;" a deed to William Penn refers to it as the Mackeriskickon. In another early document it is the "Tunikoway;" some tribes called it the "Kitbanue," or "Main Stream," and to others again it was known as the "Lamasepose," or "Fish River," because of its plentiful salmon.

Colonized by the Dutch West India Company—1630.

An ancient document exists in Amsterdam, Holland, under which patent, bearing date of July 1, 1630, Samuel Godwin and Samuel Blommaert secured title to the "Bay of the South River," otherwise the Delaware. There was a lively scramble in the old Dutch town among the members of the West India Company for large grants along the coast, including the Hudson and Delaware Rivers, and colonization was promptly begun.

The ship "Walvis," sent by Captain DeViries, arrived at the Capes early in 1631, with colonists who settled near the site of Lewiston, or Lewes, Delaware, upon a small stream called the Horekill, and also took possession of all the land in the vicinity of the Cape now called "May," in honor of the Dutch captain and explorer, Captain Cornelius Jacobsen May, for whom, also, New York Bay was long called "Port May."

The little settlement thus founded was doomed to an early extinction, for upon the following year the settlers were all massacred as the finale of a misunderstanding with the Indians.

In 1633 a Dutch Commissary, Arendt Corssen, bought a tract of land upon the Schuylkill River, establishing there a trading post. Soon after certain English colonists from Virginia undertook to effect a lodgment upon the Delaware, but were captured and sent back whence they came.

Swedish Colonists—1638.

The spring of 1638 witnessed the arrival upon the Delaware or (South) River of a new element in the form of an expedition sent out by the Swedish West India Company, and piloted by Peter Minuit, a former director of the Dutch Company. Their two ships, the "Key of Calmar" and the "Griffin," sailed up the river as far as the site of the City of Wilmington, bestowing upon the stream at that point, called by the Dutch the "Minqua's Kill," the name of their Queen, "Christina," since corrupted to "Christiana."

Having made a treaty with the Indians and built their fort, called also Christina, they were in nominal control of the west shore of the river from Cape Henlopen to the falls at the site of Trenton, although Fort Nassau, a Dutch stronghold, was located about four miles below the site of the city built by Penn half a century later upon the New Jersey shore.* Nevertheless, the two peoples dwelt together with but little friction and prospered.

OLD SWEDES CHURCH, PHILADELPHIA.

The Swedes had at this time also established a settlement at "Wicaco," now a densely populated section of the City of Philadelphia.

Early in 1641, an English colony from New Haven, Connecticut, under Robert Cogswell, came to the South River and founded a town on Varcken's Kill, now Salem Creek, and another upon the Schuylkill.† Against these interlopers the Dutch and Swedes joined forces, and drove them back to Yankee land.

---

* Fort Nassau was built upon the New Jersey shore, near the mouth of Timber Creek, not far from Gloucester, and Fort Beversrede was located upon the west bank of the Schuylkill, near the famous Bartram's Garden, now one of the parks of the City of Philadelphia. Its site was upon a point of rocks near the deep cut of the P. W. & B. R. R. The Swedes afterwards neutralized the value of this fort by building another and a stronger one at the mouth of the Schuylkill, which, with that of New Gottenburg at Tinicum Island, Fort Christina at Christina Creek, and Fort Elfsborg at Salem Creek, gave them control over New Sweden, which extended from the head of navigation, near Trenton, to Cape Henlopen.

† A Dutch word meaning "Hidden Creek."

First Organized Government within Limits of Pennsylvania—Tinicum—1643.

1643 brought to the colony of the Swedes that ponderous character Lieutenant John Printz, as Governor for the Crown, backed by the war ships "Swan" and "Charitas," as well as a shipload of new colonists. Printz selected the island of "Tenacong," now "Tinicum," as his capital, and built there his fort, "New Gottenburg," and his mansion of state, which has come down in the romance of the time as "Printz Hall." The old Quarantine and the club houses at Tinicum are near the site of this, the first capital of organized government in the limits of the State of Pennsylvania. The waters of the river have long ago swallowed up the exact site of the Swedish buildings of state, but it is said that ancient bricks are occasionally found along the shores at low tide which once had a place in their walls.

Capture of Fort Christina by Stuyvesant—1655.

Against the aggressive, and often insolent, nature of Governor John Printz, the quiet-loving Dutchmen could not long prevail or remain at peace with their neighbors. Appealing, therefore, to the greater and stronger Dutch colony upon Manhattan Island, they were gladdened, in 1651, by a visit from Peter Stuyvesant, from New Amsterdam, who having thus informed himself of the situation, proceeded, in leisurely Dutch fashion, to checkmate John Printz. It was the son-in-law and successor of Governor Printz, however, John Pappegoya, who saw the fleet of Stuyvesant, seven bulky ships, with over six hundred determined men, whose "Dutch was up," come sailing up the river, in September, 1655, to invest and capture Fort Christina, and forever dispel the dream of a new Sweden in America.

The Holland Patent—New Castle as the Capital.

From the time of that expedition the Dutch flag floated long unchallenged upon the shores of the river. A portion of the lands of the Dutch West India Company were sold to discharge a heavy debt to the City of Amsterdam, this transaction covering the shore of the river from Christina Creek to Bombay Hook. This "colony of the city" was called Nieuwer Amstel, from a suburb of the Dutch metropolis, and as a capital "Casimir" (now New Castle) was founded. Fort Christina became "Altona," and the Swedish capital was changed to "Island Kattenburg."

Old Swedish Churches.

Many of the Swedish agriculturists remained contentedly upon the river, leaving as monuments of their time which endure to the present day two substantial and picturesque churches, the "Old Swedes" of Wilmington, and the "Old Swedes" of Philadelphia, in the district of "Southwark" or "Wicaco," in whose little graveyards rest the dust of many a gallant man and woman, pioneers upon whose foundations the Anglo-Saxon came and built the great empire of the West.

Philadelphia Planned by William Penn—1681—Rapid Growth of the Young City—Penn's Second Visit and Subsequent Misfortunes.

The Dutch authorities at Manhattan surrendered to the English in 1664, upon which the town was rechristened "New York;" and in October of the same year a fleet, under Sir Robert Carre, invested and captured by assault Fort Trinity, at Christina, and held the balance of power upon the Delaware thereafter; except for a brief period preceding the cession of all their American possessions by the Hollanders to the English, in 1674.

William Penn, already a proprietor of a portion of the Province of New Jersey, now gained, through the influence of his father, Admiral William Penn, the Charter of Pennsylvania from Charles II, which was given, with ample powers, upon March 4, 1681, at Westminster. Penn's cousin, Captain William Markham, of the British army, was dispatched to inaugurate the new order of things. He was followed by three Commissioners, William Crispin,* John Bezar, and Nathaniel Allen, to lay out a city to be called Philadelphia; and with the help of Thomas Fairman, an English surveyor, who lived in Shackamaxon, north of the proposed town, it was duly laid out. Three counties, Philadelphia, Bucks and Chester, were created upon the arrival of the proprietor, in person, in October, 1682. Having, after nearly two years of effort, established a healthy impetus and order in his new city, Penn returned to England to meet troublous times. King Charles having died, James II, his successor, a monarch under Romanist influences, required much conciliation; the after result of which was to cause the proprietor, in the reign of William and Mary, much loss and long imprisonment. His province was taken from him, but restored in 1694, but it was not until 1699 that he once more set eyes upon his beloved Philadelphia. In the interim of his absence,

PENN'S SEAL.

* The first-named commissioner was a brother-in-law of Admiral Penn, and himself a distinguished naval officer, descended from an old French family. Silas Crispin, his son, came to Philadelphia in 1682, and married the daughter of Thomas Holmes, his father's successor. His second wife was the daughter of Richard Stockton, of New Jersey. Numerous descendants are now among our local population.

THE PENN TREATY. [From the Painting at rooms of the Historical Society.]

upwards of seven hundred houses had been built, with streets, shops, warehouses, meeting houses and wharves, with a population of 4,500 souls. Further complications in England called the proprietor home in October, 1701. William Penn became an insolvent debtor despite his vast possessions, and in 1708 was confined in the Fleet Prison, under the cruel debtor laws of the time. Soon afterward his health failed, and he died in 1718. The government of Pennsylvania was vested in the Penn family until the War of the Revolution, which put an end to all authority emanating from the British Crown.

OLD BLUE ANCHOR TAVERN.

Penn's Treaty.

Not far from the group of vast iron-clads gathered at the splendid Cramp's shipyard, is the little water-side Park marking the scene of the historic landing of William Penn and of his highly successful "dicker" with the sons of the forest. The old Treaty Tree, as seen in the painting at the rooms of the Historical Society, was a wide-spreading elm, which finally succumbed to the elements in 1810, and the location of which was marked by a long-neglected monument, erected in 1827. In October, 1893, the Bramble Club, of Kensington, a very lively and patriotic organization, celebrated the 211th anniversary of the event by a realistic "landing," which has been described by that graphic writer, Mr. Joel Cook, of the *Ledger*, as follows:

"The landing and treaty were all acted out to the letter. The good ship 'Welcome' sailed briskly up the river, with wind and tide favoring, and rounding-to, dropped anchor off the Park. The Indians were in force on the shore, with their tents and camp-fires. Penn and his companions landed. There was Penn, in broad brimmed hat and long coat, wearing a bright blue sash; Markham, in brilliant scarlet coat, cocked hat and epaulettes, and the Swede Lasse Cock, the interpreter, in leather breeches and fur coat, who is described in history as 'speaking an indescribable mixture of Swedish, Dutch, English and Indian.' Their party brought large chests with them, while the Indians stood stolidly gazing in a group about the great Tamanend, in his long, flowing white hair. The interpreter, after some trouble, brought them together, and they squatted in a semicircle around the fire and smoked the pipe of peace. Then Penn gave them gifts out of the chests, whereat they marvelled much, and they made their treaty, in imitation of the famous compact of Shackamaxon, an alliance of peace and friendship; the only treaty, said Voltaire, which was 'never sworn to and never broken.'

"Penn, before his arrival, in his instruction to 'be tender of offending the Indians,' had further written: 'To soften them to me and the people, let them know you are come to sit down lovingly beside them. Let my letter and conditions with my purchasers, about just dealing with them, be read in their tongue, that they may see we

STEAMSHIP INDIANA DEPARTING UPON THE RUSSIAN RELIEF EXPEDITION.

have their good in our eye, equal with our own interest, and after reading my letter and the said conditions, then present their kings with what I send them, and make a friendship and league with them, according to these conditions, which carefully observe and get them to comply with. From time to time, in my name and for my use buy land of them. Thus careful was the founder in his original dealings with the Indians, so that it is not surprising after he saw Philadelphia he was so much pleased that he wrote: 'As to outward things we are satisfied, the land good, the air clear and sweet, the springs plentiful, and provision good and easy to come at, an innumerable quantity of wild fowl and fish; in fine, here is what an Abraham, Isaac and Jacob would be well contented with, and service enough for God, for the fields here are white for harvest. Oh, how sweet is the quiet of these parts, freed from the anxious and troublesome solicitations, hurries and perplexities of woeful Europe.'"

Philadelphia the National Capital.

The century following Penn's second visit witnessed the development of his "greene country towne," beside the Delaware, into the capitol of a young nation, and its constant growth in importance until at the commencement of the nineteenth century it held a population of 67,811 persons, with a tributary country filled with a thrifty agricultural people composed of descendants of all the elements which had once contended for the mastery of the rich land we still call "Pennsylvania," and the neighboring States.

A Great Industrial Metropolis.

It has remained for the genius of the century now nearly closed, to create from the good beginning thus outlined, a great industrial metropolis of more than a million souls, the abode of prosperity, comfort, learning, invention and "brotherly love," for which the peaceful Delaware River is the gateway to all the world beyond the seas.

Birth-Place of Steam Navigation.

It is to the everlasting glory of the Delaware River that the problem of steam navigation was first tried and brought to a successful result upon her waters. John Fitch experimented, upon July 20, 1786, with a small boat operated with a steam engine, and upon August 22, 1787, he moved a boat forty feet long, by steam, with paddle wheels. In 1788, a steamboat ran from Philadelphia to Burlington, N. J., at the rate of four miles an hour, and the following year the speed was doubled, the boat making a distance of 3,000 miles during the season. A steamboat was finished with a stern wheel by Oliver Evans, in 1804, which made sixteen miles per hour; and in 1807-8-9, the walking-beam steamer John C. Stevens ran regularly between Philadelphia and Burlington, N. J.

Historic Landmarks.

There are to-day, along the river shores, many places and features of deep historic interest. Starting at Tacony, there is the old wharf where, in the palmy days of the Camden and Amboy Railroad, the New York passengers were brought by steamer for transfer to the train, prior to the completion of the great Trenton bridge and the railroad via Bristol.

Over upon the Jersey side is the " Pea Shore " and the little Tammany Fish House, famous for its punch.

A mile below Cramp's Ship Yard is moored the School Ship " Saratoga," an old-time frigate, the floating acadamy of young tars, Philadelphia boys, many of whom could take a merchantman safely across the Atlantic, or handle a gun's crew like veterans in a sea fight. At Race Street Wharf the old warship "St. Louis" is moored as the armory for the Naval Reserves of this port, an influential and enthusiastic body of young men.*

The old Navy Yard, established in 1801, near the foot of Washington avenue, where many a great wooden wall was launched, and where workers swarmed like bees during the Civil War, has long since disappeared in favor of League Island.

Battle of Red Bank.

Before bidding adieu to historical topics, some allusion should be made to the battle of Red Bank and the naval attack upon Fort Mifflin, events connected with the British occupation of Philadelphia during the war of the Revolution.

In October, 1777, the British were in full possession of the city, while the Continental troops held the country roundabout and had also closed the navigation of the Delaware River by heavy obstructions, which were protected by Mud Fort, now Fort Mifflin, and the fort at Red Bank. To effect a junction of their army and naval fleet it was necessary for the invaders to capture these works. Upon October 21st Count Donop, a young colonel of Hessians, with his grenadiers and chasseurs, crossed the river in boats and marched to the attack of the Red Bank Fort, which was held by Rhode Islanders. Although the enemy outnumbered the defenders about eight to one, they were defeated with the loss of their commander and four hundred killed and wounded. Count Donop was buried on the field, the spot being still marked. The battlefield is now a national reservation.

Siege of Fort Mifflin.

Upon the following day the naval fight began, with the loss of the frigates "Augusta" and "Merlin," which burned and exploded. The British then erected batteries upon the Schuylkill shore, commanding the

---

* See articles upon School Ship and Naval Reserves.

rear and flank of the fort upon Mud Island. From September 27th to October 16th, the little garrison of about three hundred men held out against half-a-dozen frigates, aggregating two hundred and forty guns, besides floating batteries, armed barges and shore batteries. At the end of this time there were but forty men left who were able to retreat to the shelter of Red Bank, after one of the most gallant episodes in the history of warfare.

Philadelphia's Water Front.

The water front of the City of Philadelphia, extending along the Delaware River and upon both shores of the Schuylkill River, as far as the dam at the Fairmount Water Works, has an extent for shipping and naval purposes of thirty-four miles. That portion of the Schuylkill above Walnut Street bridge being accessible only to barges and tugs. To this ample space should be added the wharfage room of the opposite City of Camden, N. J., amounting to six miles. Less than half this distance is now occupied by the improvements incident to the present volume of commerce and extent of manufactures abutting upon the water front. The gradual utilization of all of this priceless shore line is the constant concern of The Philadelphia Maritime Exchange, and other commercial bodies, whose united efforts and intelligent foresight must do much to hasten the natural growth and improvement of this source of the city's wealth and greatness. Attention is also directed to the fact that for a distance of many miles north of the northern limits of this city there is a depth at low water of not less than fifteen feet.

The great institutions and industries ranged along the Delaware River front of Philadelphia almost continuously for twelve miles include: The House

READING RAILROAD COAL TERMINAL AT PORT RICHMOND.

of Correction, at Holmesburg; the Disston Saw Works, Tacony; the Tacony Iron and Metal Works, where the great statue of William Penn was cast; the United States Arsenal, at Bridesburg; the grain elevators and Reading Railroad coal terminal, at Port Richmond; the great ship building plant of William Cramp & Sons, at Kensington; the ship building and marine engine establishment of Neafie & Levy, at Kensington; the many wharves and warehouses of the foreign and coastwise steamship and sailing vessel lines ranged in front of the old city proper; the terminals for transshipment of freight of the several great railroad corporations; the ferries to the New Jersey shore; the towering sugar refineries; large chemical works; coal piers of the Pennsylvania Railroad, at Greenwich Point; and at League Island, the United States Navy Yard, destined, from its many natural advantages, to become the greatest Government naval rendezvous for constructing and repair work, recruiting and other necessities of the navy of the future, upon either the Atlantic or Pacific seaboard.*

The annual report of Commodore George W. Melville, Chief of the Bureau of Steam Engineering, issued October, 1894, contains the following emphatic sentence in regard to League Island Navy Yard: "Too much cannot be urged in favor of completing this yard in compliance with the recommendations in the very excellent report of the board composed of Captains Potter, Farquhar and Whitehead, and Civil Engineers Endicott and Peary, United States Navy, who went over the whole matter exhaustively, and prepared plans that, if carried out, give the United States a naval station second to none in the world. The advantages of location and surroundings are too well known to need repetition. In short, there is every good reason why this should be the principal naval station for building, repairing and laying up modern ships, and not one against it."

---

* See article and map regarding League Island.

Upon the Schuylkill borders of the city is located, at Girard Point, a group of large grain elevators, and two miles above, at Point Breeze, is the immense oil refining industry and oil shipping terminal, around which are always clustered a forest of masts of ships awaiting foreign and coastwise cargoes of this Pennsylvania commodity. Still further up the Schuylkill are the wharves of numerous chemical works, abattoirs, marble and granite works, cement, tile and brick and mortar works, with various other large interests.

Upon the Camden side of the river are the ship yards at Cooper's Point and Kaighn's Point, and the several terminals of the railroads to the seashore. Opposite Greenwich Point, and just above Gloucester, N. J., is the extensive plant of the Gloucester Manufacturing Company.

Advantages for Manufacturers.

Much space might be devoted profitably to the presentation of the many advantages to be gained by manufacturers of nearly all kinds of goods in building their factories at or near the still unoccupied river margins already referred to within the limits of Philadelphia. The project of a continuous Belt Line Railway for freight, completely encircling the city and connecting at convenient points with all of the railroad lines entering the city, is already partially realized. The abundance of coal within the limits of Pennsylvania; a great and permanent population of skilled workers, largely owning their homes; local rapid transit to all sections of the city; the lesser distance, as compared with New York and the New England factory centres, to all large Western cities; the economy of shipment by water to this port of the almost untouched forest and mining wealth of the South; the banking facilities; the healthful latitude of the region—these are valid claims upon the attention of the far-sighted investor, and especially to one who hopes for a lodgement in the foreign market for his goods.

Nearly forty per cent. of the entire population of the United States is found within a radius of three hundred miles of Philadelphia, and a circle drawn around the city at that distance includes or enters fourteen States.

In the past the commerce of the city has been vastly aided by a number of canals linking the waters of the Delaware with other navigable estuaries of the seaboard. The Delaware and Raritan canal extends from Bordentown, N. J., upon the Delaware River, to New Brunswick, N. J., upon the Raritan River, a distance of forty-four miles; and the Chesapeake and Delaware Canal connects the two bays of the name by a ten-foot channel, fourteen miles long. Although these channels in their present condition are far from adequate to the requirements of the enlarged dimensions of modern marine carriers, it has been recently demonstrated that light draught war vessels of the gunboat type may be rapidly taken through them when required.

Removal of the Islands.

The most important work in progress at the present time, is the removal of the islands, which formerly occupied much space, immediately opposite the heart of the city; an undertaking now well advanced by the American Dredging Company, under their contract with the general government. This operation includes the removal of Smith's and Windmill Islands, and a part of Petty's Island and adjacent shoals. The work is under the supervision of Maj. C. W. Raymond, of the Corps of U. S. Engineers, whose district also includes the channels of the Delaware to the sea, which it is confidently expected will be further deepened and increased in width at an early time.*

The Pennsylvania and New Jersey Railroad Company's Bridge Across the Delaware River.

Work upon this great undertaking, designed to give direct railroad service between Philadelphia and points in central and southern New Jersey, has been commenced according to the plans adopted by the Government. It will span the Delaware River between the suburb of Bridesburg, at Roxborough Street, and Fisher's Point, Camden, N. J. The length between shore piers is 1,950 feet, with a draw of 300 feet width. The elevation above high water line is 50 feet. A determined effort has been made by public organizations in Philadelphia to secure a greater elevation than that fixed upon, but Congress has failed to take such action as would result in the desired modification.

Description of the Quarantine Station of the State of Pennsylvania.

The Quarantine Station of the State of Pennsylvania is located at Essington, Delaware County, about ten miles southwest of Philadelphia. It is conveniently reached by the B. & O. R. R., from Twenty-fourth and Chestnut streets to Essington, and the P. R. R. from Broad street Station to Moore's, a quarter of a mile and two miles respectively from the gates of the Quarantine Station.

The Station comprises altogether sixteen acres of land; of these six belong to the United States Government, but have for many years been used in conjunction with the adjoining ten acres which constitute the grounds of the Quarantine Station proper.

On the Quarantine Station proper, the aforesaid ten acres, are located a number of buildings. The Main, or Administration Building, is 50 feet square, built of brick in the year 1798, very solidly constructed, and altogether a very handsome building. It contains twelve rooms, each 20 by

---
* See Annual Report of the Philadelphia Maritime Exchange for 1894, Appendix R. Also Reports of U. S. Engineer in charge, and the chapter upon another page regarding harbor improvements.

24 feet, and ceilings 10 feet high; bath, water-closets, store-rooms, three large attics and two large kitchens. This building is heated throughout by steam, and is occupied by the Superintendent of the Station and his family.

Adjoining the Main Building on either side are wings 65 feet by 26 feet wide, two-and-one-half stories high, each containing six rooms, each room 22 by 27 feet, ceilings 10 feet high. Each wing is provided with bath-rooms and water-closets. The plumbing fixtures are all of the most approved modern sanitary kind. At the end of each wing is a kitchen. In front, and on either side of the Main Building, 120 feet distant therefrom, are located smaller substantially built brick buildings, the one to the west being at present occupied by one of the Deputy Quarantine Physicians as a dwelling, and the one to the east is temporarily occupied by the crew of the boarding tug. These houses are 48 feet by 24 feet, two-and-one-half stories high, have seven rooms and two attics each, and have ceilings 11 feet high. They are provided with bath and water-closet appliances of the most approved sanitary plumbing.

The Hospital proper is located northwest of the Main Building, about 300 feet distant therefrom. It is 72 feet long by 24 feet wide, two stories in height, contains two wards on the first floor, each 22 by 22 feet, ceilings 10 feet high, and these are exactly duplicated on the second floor, which also contains a Nurse's room, Dispensary, Bath-room, and Water-closet, all of the best modern plumbing work. Adjoining, on the west side of the Hospital Building, is a Kitchen, 16 by 24 feet, and on the east a similar building, which is used as a dead-room or Morgue.

A Stable and Carriage-house, 70 by 40 feet, is situated to the northwest of the main building, about 100 feet distant therefrom. On the grounds are also a Laundry and Wash-house, 30 by 12 feet; a Store-house for disinfectants, 16 feet square; a substantially built Power-house over an artesian well, 12 feet square, and an Ice-house, 30 feet square.

Upon the Government property adjoining is a Barrack built of stone, 150 feet long by 40 feet wide, two-and-one-half stories high, each floor divided into two main rooms, 74 by 28 feet each. The large room to the east has been subdivided into three, two equal-sized rooms having been fitted up as large bath-rooms, each bath-room containing twelve tubs abundantly supplied with hot and cold water, and heated by steam.

Projecting southward from the Government property is a pier, which was in a very dilapidated condition at the time that the State Quarantine Board leased the plant. Recently the Board has expended about $900 on this pier and the dock adjoining to the east. On this wharf are located a steam disinfectant plant, 15 feet square, a Power-house adjoining the same, and which contains a twenty-five horse-power upright boiler of recent make. The disinfecting house proper is a frame building, and although erected as a temporary structure, is well constructed and well braced. It is built of two thicknesses of yellow pine siding with felt between, and is lined throughout with the best quality of tin, all joints being soldered. In this building a temperature of between 215 and 220 degrees Fahrenheit has frequently been obtained for a period of four hours without intermission. On this pier are also located large coal bins, which, at the time of this writing, are charged with 300 tons of pea coal. The Station is equipped with cots, bedding, bed clothing, etc., sufficient for the immediate accommodation of 500 persons, and the unoccupied portions of the land are ample to accommodate 200 suspects. There are also about 100 wall tents and floors in good condition and immediately available.

The entire property is thoroughly underdrained. There is not a well or cesspool of any description on the place, the drainage being carried out to the river below low water mark through a sewer constructed at great expense. All dejections and discharges from patients, before being emptied into the sewer, are thoroughly disinfected.

The water supply is clean and pure, and is obtained from an artesian well, 300 feet deep, the water being pumped out by a hot-air engine into a tank (3,000 gallons capacity) in the Main Building, and thence it is distributed throughout the entire place.

On the first floor of the east wing of the Main Building there is an apparatus for the disinfection of mail. It consists of a sheet iron box with double walls and double doors. Within the chamber are a number of iron wire trays. The inside measurements are $3\frac{1}{2}$ by 3 by $2\frac{1}{2}$ feet. It is heated by alcohol, and a temperature of between 300 and 400 degrees dry heat can be maintained for an indefinite time. All letters treated in this chamber are marked "sterilized," and forwarded.

The facilities for anchorage of vessels is good. In the channel between Little Tinicum Island and the Station there is from 20 to 26 feet of water, but the width of the channel is not sufficient to allow large vessels to swing at cable, but smaller vessels can safely be anchored therein. In the main channel between Little Tinicum Island and the New Jersey shore there is excellent anchorage for the largest vessels that come to this port.

Attached to the Quarantine Station is a boarding tug, the "Lizzie Crawford," which is manned by five men :—captain, engineer, fireman, steward and deck-hand, who are all neatly uniformed. A feature of this boarding tug is two shelves or platforms, built at the suggestion of Dr. Boenning, the Quarantine Physician. These shelves are each 20 feet long by $2\frac{1}{2}$ feet wide; they project from the sides of the upper deck of the tug. They are strongly braced and immensely facilitate the work of boarding a vessel in stream, and at the same time materially contribute to the safety of the boarding officials.

The mail facilities are good, there being one delivery at the Station every day from Moore's or the post-office at Essington.

The Quarantine Station is supplied with a very efficient Telephone Service, costing the Board $1,250 per year. It consists of a metallic circuit from the Station to the Telephone Exchange at Fourth and Market Streets, and connects with any instrument of the general system or any long-distance instrument at any point. The office of the Quarantine Physician is supplied with a similar instrument, and also the office of the State Quarantine Board, thereby insuring a most satisfactory means of communication between the Quarantine Station and the city at all times. There is also in the office building at the Quarantine Station a telegraph apparatus, which, however, at present is detached.

The personnel of the Quarantine Station consists of Dr. Boenning, Quarantine Physician, who is the Executive Officer under the law; two Deputy Quarantine Physicians, appointed by the Quarantine Physician, Drs. William Shimer and Alfred M. Seymour; the Superintendent, Mr. H. L. McLaughlin, and a number of employés, among whom are nurses and laborers. All of the foregoing, except the Quarantine Physician himself, reside at the Quarantine Station permanently.

The State Quarantine Service is conducted under the law of the State of Pennsylvania of June 5, 1893, and is also in harmony with the United States Quarantine Laws. All Quarantine regulations are vigorously carried out, both in letter and spirit. It has been the aim of the Quarantine Physician not to afflict the commerce of the port by any undue detention.

The Quarantine Service of the State is in force throughout the year.

The only vessels exempt from the inspection of the Quarantine officials are those from United States ports north of Cape Henry. If, however, it is deemed advisable by the Quarantine Physician to board any vessel from any port he is empowered under the statute so to do.

The inspection of a vessel consists in the careful examination of the crew and passengers; inspection of the water supply, water-closets, and the general sanitary condition of the ship. The treatment of a vessel in Quarantine is in accordance with the Rules and Regulations of the Board, and as the Quarantine Physician directs.

Communication with vessels in Quarantine is by means of the Quarantine Physician and his Deputies by the boarding tug. No inter-communication is allowed between vessels in quarantine.

Any vessel infected with Cholera, Yellow Fever, or Small Pox, will be energetically dealt with and as directed with the Rules and Regulations of the Board and the Treasury Department, and supplemented by any special directions which may, in the judgment of the Quarantine Physician, be necessary thoroughly to meet all conditions that may arise.

A perfect series of records are kept, in compliance with the Act of Assembly, of June 5, 1893.

The Health Officer of the City of Philadelphia collects the following fees: Any steamship arriving from a foreign port pays a fee of ten dollars; all sailing vessels arriving from a foreign port pay a fee of five dollars; all coasting vessels, sail or steam, arriving from a port of the United States, south of the St. Mary River, Florida, pay a fee of two dollars and fifty cents. There are no fees or expenses of any kind incurred by vessels in quarantine, all of the expense of maintenance, disinfection, etc., being borne by the State.

During the year ending June 30, 1894, 1578 vessels were inspected and passed at this Quarantine. The commerce of the port is of the most varied character.

The Quarantine Service of the State of Pennsylvania is under the direction of a Board of seven members.

The State Quarantine Station may be reached by rail from Twenty-fourth and Chestnut Streets Depot, over the Chester branch of the Reading Railroad, in about a half hour.

IRON PIER AT CAPE HENLOPEN.

Inauguration of the National Quarantine System upon the Delaware.

Imported pestilence and contagion brought in ships from the ports of the South, have, in years gone by, found but a slight barrier upon the Delaware River to resist their lodgment among the people along its shores. The long-established quarantine station at Tinicum, known as the "Lazaretto," has no doubt contributed largely to the prevention of a repetition of the dread scenes in Philadelphia incident to the yellow fever epidemics in 1802 and 1820, or the cholera ravages of 1832. This establishment, maintained by the State of Pennsylvania, and continued under the new law of July, 1893, co-operates effectively with the new station, completed and conducted by the general government, which is located at Reedy Island, forty-five miles below Philadelphia, and the quarantine at Cape Henlopen.

Recognizing the fact that the average citizen is usually entirely uninformed regarding the costly and elaborate preparations made for his safety in anticipation of epidemic years, and that even business men engaged in maritime matters are often but inadequately posted in regard to the subject, we give liberal space to a full description of the two "plants" now in operation under the care of medical sentinels, faithful to their duty as guards set at our outer portals. It is believed that the Delaware River quarantine is now the most complete existing in the United States.

Conceding the valuable aid and co-operation of the commercial bodies of Philadelphia in securing this splendid result, it may be safely claimed that the credit is chiefly due, for the new order of things as detailed in the following pages, to The Philadelphia Maritime Exchange; firstly, in urging upon the people and the authorities the danger of a repetition of the visit of cholera to our shores as in 1892, and, secondly, in aiding the government officer in immediate charge of the work, Surgeon-General Walter Wyman, of the Marine Hospital Service, by every means in its power, entailing upon the officers and committees of the Exchange a large amount of personal attention, which has been cheerfully given whenever required.

DELAWARE BREAKWATER QUARANTINE STATION—EXECUTIVE BUILDING AND SURGEON'S QUARTERS.

United States Quarantine System on the Delaware Bay and River.

Delaware Breakwater Station.

The Delaware Breakwater Quarantine Station, at the mouth of the Delaware Bay, was established by the national government in 1884, and was opened on the 1st of August of that year. It was established upon the recommendation of the then senior Senator of Delaware, and by request of the authorities of Philadelphia, Pa., and Wilmington and Lewes, Del., and, until the passage of the Act of February 15, 1893, was operated *in aid* of the local quarantines on the Delaware Bay and River.

The reservation has a water front of 1,500 feet and a depth of 1,200 feet, and is situated one-half a mile distant from the tip of Cape Henlopen, between the cape and the town of Lewes. Of this reservation, the greater portion—900 feet on the sea front running back 1,090 feet—is surrounded by a board fence eight feet in height, enclosing all the quarantine buildings except the surgeon's quarters and boat house. About 900 feet from the western boundary of the reservation is an iron pier 1,701 feet in length, with a width at the shore end of 21 feet, while the outer 546 feet have a width of 42 feet. This was erected by the Engineer Department of the army at a total cost of about $368,500. Provisional transfer of the pier was made to the Marine Hospital Service by Congress in 1890. The depth of water at the end of this pier is 25 feet.

DELAWARE BREAKWATER QUARANTINE STATION—BARRACKS, BATH HOUSE, LAVATORIES AND SMALLER HOSPITAL.

The surgeon's quarters, as stated above, are without the quarantine enclosure, and are two stories in height and built of brick. They contain the administration offices also. The whole building is well finished and comfortably fitted up throughout, and contains fifteen rooms.

The boat house, 48 x 18 feet, is a short distance from the surgeon's quarters, nearer the shore line.

Within the enclosure are the two hospitals, steward's quarters, barracks for detained immigrants, dining rooms and kitchen for same, bath house, disinfecting chamber, laundry, boiler house and artesian well.

The hospitals, two in number and some 600 feet apart, are both situated on the sea front, and the larger one, 60 x 30 feet, two stories in height, includes an addition just completed, increasing the quarters for the hospital steward on duty at the quarantine station. This hospital has a capacity of about twenty beds, while the smaller one, 50 x 30 feet, can afford accommodation for about twelve patients.

The immigrant bath house is 86 x 16 feet, with an addition 24 x 16 feet on each end. The bath house contains twenty shower baths and one bath tub, with hot and cold water connections to each bath. The additions contain disrobing and dressing rooms. The boiler house and laundry, twenty feet distant from the bath house, is 61 feet 6 inches in length by 21 feet in breadth, and is divided into two rooms. The one next the bath house contains the steam disinfecting chamber, constructed by the Kensington Engine Works after designs furnished by Passed Assistant Surgeon J. J. Kinyoun, M. H. S. The steam chamber is intended only for the disinfection of wearing apparel of immigrants detained for observation and sickness. It is 4 feet 4 inches by 5 feet 4 inches by 9 feet 6 inches in dimensions, and has two cars which support wire screens upon which the articles to be disinfected are spread before being run into the chamber. The cars run on an iron track, a section of which, sufficient in length to support the car, is itself movable, and can be brought either to join the track entering the chamber, or to the one running alongside. The boiler house also contains the boiler for generating steam to be used for disinfecting and for running a small engine and pump. The other half of the building, the laundry, contains

DELAWARE BREAKWATER QUARANTINE STATION—KITCHEN.

DELAWARE BREAKWATER QUARANTINE STATION—STEAM DISINFECTING CHAMBER.

DELAWARE BREAKWATER QUARANTINE STATION—BOILER HOUSE AND LAUNDRY, BATH HOUSE, AND ONE WING OF BARRACKS—(LOOKING NORTH).

twenty-four stationary wash tubs and drying apparatus for the use of the detained immigrants. These two buildings were erected in 1893.

The barracks, which are the next buildings to those just described, consist of two structures, each 300 x 24 feet, and of a clear height of 12 feet. One runs nearly north and south and the other nearly east and west. They are each divided by five partitions into compartments of equal size, and contain accommodations for from 800 to 1000 immigrants. The bunks are arranged in tiers, three in number, and are similar in arrangement to those in the steerage of a vessel carrying immigrants. Each barrack has an addition, 15 x 44 feet in dimensions, containing rooms for nurses and storerooms for sheets, pillows, etc. The barracks are not connected, but in the interval between them is the building containing the dining room for immigrants, kitchen and storerooms. This building is 48 feet square, with an addition 18 x 45 feet. The kitchen contains apparatus for cooking by steam, and all the most modern appliances for the speedy preparation of food for large numbers of people.

In the rear of the barracks are found the latrines, 30 x 10 feet, with a height of 9 feet. Water is supplied to all these buildings by an artesian well situated within the enclosure, and driven to a depth of 394 feet. With the use of a pump the daily output of this well—per day of twenty-four hours—is from 18,000 to 21,000 gallons, a quantity sufficient for all purposes required. The water is carried by overhead piping to the buildings, and to two large tanks situated near the bath house, and which can be seen in the photograph of same.

All the buildings within the enclosure are constructed of wood, and are connected with one another and with the surgeon's quarters by boardwalks.

As will be observed by the above description of Delaware Breakwater Quarantine, it is fitted up as a place of detention for suspects, and for those actually suffering from some quarantinable disease; but as yet nothing has been said about the treatment of the vessel that may have brought such suspects or ill immigrants. Before the summer of 1893, the only vessels

REEDY ISLAND STATION, NATIONAL QUARANTINE.
THE PHILADELPHIA MARITIME EXCHANGE REPORTING STATION IS TOWER.

required to stop for inspection at Delaware Breakwater were those coming from an infected port, or having at time of arrival a disease of a quarantinable character on board. All other vessels were treated at the Philadelphia local quarantine. Disinfection of vessels at the Breakwater was practiced by introducing the disinfectant, sulphur, usually, from a disinfecting tug laid alongside. But the threatened invasion of cholera during the summer of 1892 made it necessary for all vessels from foreign ports to be rigidly inspected at the Breakwater, and it was found that the carrying out of this order entailed great hardship on all concerned. The anchorage at the Breakwater is almost in the open sea, and in rough weather it is sometimes impossible to board a vessel for the purpose of inspection; and, of course, the inspection, and disinfection if necessary, was frequently delayed for some time, perhaps for some days. Furthermore, a vessel arriving at Delaware Breakwater Quarantine at sundown was necessarily detained there until next morning to permit a daylight inspection, and this delay entailed considerable expense and inconvenience, as it was almost impossible for the vessel in that case to discharge her passengers in Philadelphia the same day. It became evident, for these reasons, that an additional station for inspection and disinfection of vessels was necessary, and it was moreover evident that such station should be nearer Philadelphia. Such action was urged by The Philadelphia Maritime Exchange, and also by a joint committee representing the States of Pennsylvania and Delaware, who further considered the location of the Philadelphia local quarantine, so near the City of Philadelphia, as a menace to that city. The Director of Public Safety of Philadelphia and a committee of the Pennsylvania Legislature, and others interested, called upon Surgeon-General Wyman to learn what plans he had conceived to meet the exigency of the situation, and the plans since carried into successful execution were laid before them.

Reedy Island Station.

The attention of the Surgeon-General had been, in the meantime, directed to Reedy Island as the most suitable place by an officer of the service, after consultation with an engineer officer of the army in charge of improvements in the Delaware River. Situated nearly at the junction of the Delaware Bay and River, the Government already owned the fifty acres at the northern extremity of the island, and this was turned over to the Treasury Department for quarantine purposes. The establishment of this station was urged most strongly also by the Legislature of the State of Pennsylvania, a copy of whose resolutions, forwarded by the Governor, is as follows:

Joint Resolution of Pennsylvania Legislature.

IN THE SENATE, Feb. 28, 1893.

Whereas, The President of the United States will shortly have the disposition of nearly half a million dollars for quarantine purposes;

REEDY ISLAND QUARANTINE STATION—DISINFECTING CHAMBERS AND CARS.

REEDY ISLAND QUARANTINE STATION—DISINFECTING MACHINERY, STEAM CHAMBERS AND SULPHUR FURNACE.

And Whereas, The Legislature of Pennsylvania is informed that Walter Wyman, Surgeon-General of the Marine Hospital Service, U. S. A., has strongly recommended to the Secretary of War the extension and improvement of the quarantine service at the port of Philadelphia, by establishing a boarding and disinfecting station on Reedy Island, in the Delaware River, which shall be subsidiary to the United States Marine Hospital Service at Lewes, Delaware;

And Whereas, The speedy perfection of the Federal quarantine service at the port of Philadelphia is of vital importance not only to the States bordering on the Delaware Bay and River, but to every State in the Union, inasmuch as a large majority of the immigrants landing at the port are transferred direct to other sections of the country, and the danger from the admission of contagious and infectious diseases is great; therefore be it

Resolved (If the House concur), That we, while standing ready to assist and coöperate with the Federal authorities in preventing the entrance of the threatened cholera scourge, and being determined to leave nothing undone to establish a thorough and vigilant quarantine guard at the port of Philadelphia, respectfully request the President of the United States to see to it that prompt and sufficient measures are taken to put into effect the plans of the United States Marine Hospital Service for the improvement of the quarantine system in the Delaware Bay and River; and be it further

Resolved, That the Governor of this Commonwealth be respectfully requested to communicate these resolutions to the President of the United States.

E. W. SMILEY,
Chief Clerk of the Senate.

Concurred in March 1, 1893.

CHARLES E. VOORHEES,
Chief Clerk of the House of Representatives.

Approved, this 6th day of March, A. D. 1893.

ROBT. E. PATTISON.

OFFICE OF THE
SECRETARY OF THE COMMONWEALTH.

PENNSYLVANIA, ss.:

HARRISBURG, March 10, A. D., 1893.

I do Hereby Certify, That the foregoing and annexed is a full, true and correct copy of the Original Resolution of the General Assembly of the Commonwealth of Pennsylvania, approved March 6, 1893, as the same remains on file in this office.

Seal of Secretary's Office, Pennsylvania.

In Testimony Whereof, I have hereunto set my hand and caused the Seal of the Secretary's Office to be affixed the day and year above written.

A. L. TILDEN,
Deputy Secretary of the Commonwealth.

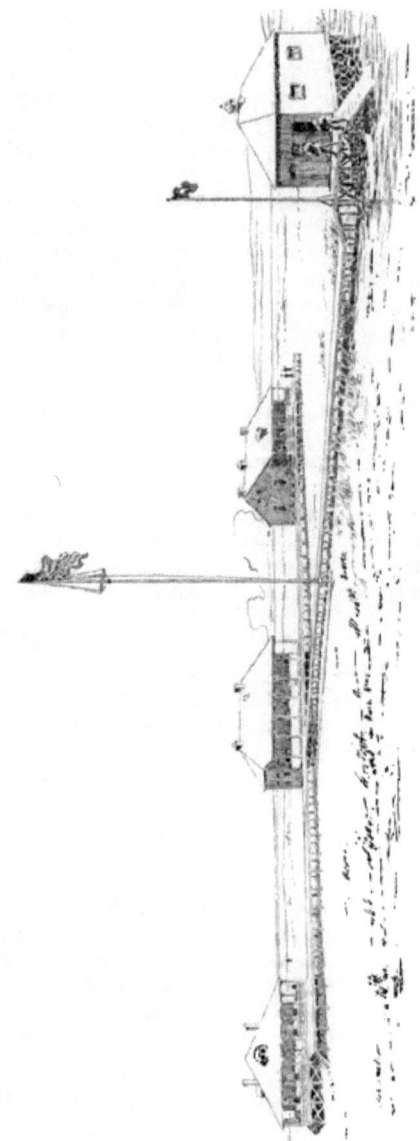

OFFICERS' QUARTERS, REEDY ISLAND STATION, NATIONAL QUARANTINE.

The site is favorable, being just above Dan Baker Shoal, so that after inspection or disinfection it is not necessary for vessels to wait for the tide to cover this bar.

An allotment was secured from the epidemic fund for the purpose of constructing and equipping this station in March, 1893, and work on the pier was begun at once; the station was opened on July 1, 1893, and at the present date is completed. The surgeon's quarters, men's quarters, cottage hospital and boat house located on Reedy Island have been constructed under contract during the past year,

The main structure of the Reedy Island Quarantine Station is the pier head and disinfecting shed. This pier, situated directly in the channel, is 200 feet long by 40 feet broad, and has a depth of water off its eastern or channel side of 30 feet at low tide. It is built of heavy piling driven down to hard bottom and firmly bolted together, and having at each end a double row of piling 50 feet long, and a triangular ice break constructed of heavy piling and timbers extending out from this double row of piling 50 feet. The depth of water off the pier allows of the mooring of a vessel directly to the pier during the process of disinfection. On this pier is the shed for the disinfecting machinery, warehouse and observatory tower, as well as quarters for attendants. The total length of the building is 196 feet; the 90 feet at the southern end being 36 feet broad, and the northern 106 feet being 23 feet broad. This latter portion is divided into warehouses and contains one large wooden tank of a capacity of 15,000 gallons. The southern portion, 90 x 36 feet, is divided into two parts, one 16 x 36 feet and one 74 x 36 feet, which contains the following disinfecting machinery: two steam chambers of the same make and pattern as the one at the Delaware Breakwater Quarantine Station already described, but larger, viz., each 15 feet long, 5 feet 4 inches high, 4 feet 4 inches in width, placed side by side, with trucks and railway. This machinery, like that at the Breakwater Quarantine Station, was designed and built by the Kensington Engine Works, Limited, of Philadelphia. The shed also contains a sulphur furnace of the Valk & Murdoch, Charleston, type, catch cylinder, exhaust fan and engine (three horse-power), to run the same, and rubber piping to conduct the fumes of SO_2 from the furnace to the vessel. A fifty horse-power boiler supplies steam for the disinfecting chambers, and in addition there is an air pump, a fire and tank pump, and another pump for the purpose of filling the bichloride tank (capacity, 3,000 gallons) which is placed on the roof. In this shed is also a tank with a capacity of 3,000 gallons.

During the past winter connection has been made between the station and the Western Union Telegraph Company lines, and to effect this a cable was laid from Port Penn across Reedy Island to the pier head. The cable is 4,800 feet in length and was laid at a cost of $1,325. An observatory has been erected on the roof of the southern end of the pier, in size, 15 feet 9 inches by 17 feet 3 inches, and fitted with telegraph instruments, so that direct telegraphic communication can now be maintained with the station.

The new buildings located on Reedy Island comprise a cottage hospital 58 x 29 feet, with a wing 19 x 14 feet; attendants' quarters, 67 feet 6 inches by 24 feet, with a veranda 67 feet 6 inches by 7 feet; and surgeon's quarters, 41 feet 2 inches by 41 feet 2 inches, with a veranda 8 feet wide all around it. These buildings are erected on piling on the island, so as to be above high water in winter and spring, and are connected by gangways. From these buildings a gangway extends 300 feet to the water, where a boat house, 49 x 28 feet, is erected on piling.

The steamer "Louis Pasteur" is used as a boarding boat at the station. She is 87 feet in length, 16 feet beam, and draws 6 feet of water. Vessels are inspected at the station between sunrise and sunset; and the distance from Philadelphia is such that a steamer inspected at Reedy Island in the morning reaches Philadelphia in time to enter and discharge passengers the same day, thus saving both time and money.

Infected vessels are, of course, as heretofore, inspected at the Breakwater, and persons exposed to infection taken off and held for observation at the Quarantine Station there, while the vessel is sent to Reedy Island for disinfection. If a vessel with quarantinable disease fails to stop at the Breakwater, as ordered to do, on inspection at Reedy Island she will be remanded to the Breakwater, if necessary; so that the contagious cases and suspected immigrants may be taken off, and she return to Reedy Island for disinfection. To quote from the report of the Secretary of the Treasury for 1893:

"With this plant at Reedy Island, and the accommodation for immigrants near the Delaware Breakwater, an efficient quarantine guard has been established for the City of Philadelphia and the other cities on the Delaware River and Bay."

Taking the station at the Breakwater and the station at Reedy Island together, there is no quarantine plant in existence superior to this. It is to be hoped that no cholera-laden vessel will arrive at the mouth of Delaware Bay, but should such a vessel appear, carrying immigrants, for example, the care and treatment of both the vessel and the immigrants would be a matter of easy and scientific administration. Those actually sick would be immediately removed to the hospital, the remaining immigrants would be immediately marched through the single gate of the inclosure to the bath house, where they would be obliged to disrobe and be given a thorough bathing, their clothing in the meantime being passed into the steam disinfecting chamber, near by. Having completed their bath, they would be given fresh clothing from the large supply of new material constantly on hand, and they would then be passed into the barracks and kept under close observation, being divided into groups for this purpose. Should cholera appear in any one group, the patient would be removed immediately to hospital, and the five days' detention of that group would begin from the date of the removal of the patient. The danger of the spread of the disease among the detained immigrants would be reduced to a minimum by reason of this grouping. The water supply is from an artesian well, which cannot by any possibility become infected.

During the season of 1893, when there was an expectation of the arrival of such a vessel at the Breakwater, an arrangement was made by the Surgeon-General with the Chief of the Revenue Cutter Service, by which between forty and fifty enlisted men would be sent from the several vessels of that service stationed in Boston, New York, Baltimore and Philadelphia, for immediate duty as guards under the command of commissioned officers.

The patients and the "suspects" being thus provided for, the vessel itself would be immediately sent to Reedy Island, where, with the perfect facilities provided, the vessel would be disinfected by fumes of sulphur thrown into its hold, the several apartments washed down with a solution of bichloride of mercury, and the dunnage of the crew and all textile fabrics disinfected by steam in the steam chambers.

No better place could be found for the detention of a large number of suspected immigrants than at the Delaware Breakwater. The high fence and the guard of the Revenue Cutter Service would effectually hold the immigrants within the enclosure, and the very fact of the remoteness of the location adds to its desirability; for it goes without saying that people affected with cholera, or suspected of being infected, cannot be too far removed from populous centres. Practically, however, the arrival of a cholera-laden ship would be a very exceptional circumstance, and the ordinary work of quarantine, namely, the inspection of vessels to find out whether they are free from disease or not, is carried on with great facility at Reedy Island. The pier, which is the boarding station, is in the direct track of vessels bound for Philadelphia, and the inspection, so far as time is concerned, is reduced to a minimum.

A still further guard in this scheme of National Quarantine on the Delaware River is the presence in Philadelphia of an experienced medical officer, Surgeon George Purviance, who is ready at any time to act as the quarantine agent of the Marine Hospital Bureau in the city. The Surgeon-General is thoroughly impressed, not only with the necessity of keeping out epidemic diseases, but also with the necessity of doing so with the least possible hampering of commerce. His policy has been constantly to so administer the regulations as to avoid all unnecessary delays or embarrassment of vessels. The transactions at these two stations during the ten months ended November 1, 1894, were as follows:

DELAWARE BREAKWATER QUARANTINE.

Vessels inspected and passed	94
Vessels inspected and ordered to Reedy Island for disinfection	7

REEDY ISLAND QUARANTINE.

Vessels inspected and passed	955
Vessels disinfected	7
Vessels spoken and passed	27
Total number of passengers inspected during the fiscal year 1894	100,000

Passed Assistant Surgeon A. H. Glennan, Marine Hospital Service, is in charge of the Reedy Island Quarantine Station, and is assisted by Sanitary Inspector A. B. McDowell; while the Delaware Breakwater Quarantine Station is under the charge of Passed Assistant Surgeon C. P. Wertenbaker, M. H. S., who was assisted during the quarantine season by Acting Assistant Surgeon W. P. Orr, since resigned.

Cost of Construction of the Stations.

THE DELAWARE BREAKWATER QUARANTINE.

Surgeon's quarters, executive offices, etc.	$16,237 00
Barracks	11,971 00
Fence	1,940 00
Bath house	2,500 00
Boiler house and laundry	2,500 00
Boilers, etc.	2,100 00
Water tanks, etc.	245 00
Steam chambers	2,115 00
Installation of same	1,423 00
Drain pipe	187 00
Artesian well	2,403 00
Pump and water distribution	2,185 00
Addition to Surgeon's quarters	1,427 00
	$47,233 00

REEDY ISLAND QUARANTINE.

Pier, with warehouse, observatory tower, disinfecting machinery, etc.	$46,422 00
Cable	1,325 00
Surgeon's quarters, cottage hospital, attendants' quarters, gangway and sewerage	19,125 00
	$66,872 00

OLD MERCHANTS' EXCHANGE BUILDING, NOW OCCUPIED BY THE PHILADELPHIA MARITIME EXCHANGE, THIRD AND WALNUT STREETS.

The Philadelphia Maritime Exchange and Its Work.

THIS representative organization was formed in March, 1875, its objects being, as defined in the charter, "to provide and regulate a suitable room or rooms for a Maritime Exchange, to acquire, preserve and disseminate all maritime and other business information, and to do such other and lawful acts as will tend to promote and encourage the commerce of the Port of Philadelphia."

Mr. William Brockie, the first President, served continuously sixteeen years.

The death of Mr. Brockie, which occurred suddenly upon September 12, 1890, while upon his way to his office, was deeply mourned by not only this organization, but thousands of business men and many other commercial bodies with which he was identified. Mr. Brockie was born in Edinburgh, in 1834, and long represented the Allan Line of steamships in this city. His portrait, a splendid work in oil, purchased by popular subscription, adorns the eastern wall of The Maritime Exchange rotunda.

In 1891 Mr. A. C. Ferguson was elected to the Presidency, and re-elected in 1892. Mr. George E. Earnshaw was elected President in 1893, and is in office at the present time, having also been re-elected.

The following are the officers and committees for 1894 and 1895:

President,
GEO. E. EARNSHAW.

Vice-President,
THOMAS WINSMORE.

Treasurer,
DAVID S. STETSON.

Honorary Vice-President,
PHILIP FITZPATRICK.

Secretary,
E. R. SHARWOOD.

Assistant Secretary,
ELISHA CROWELL.

Solicitor,
JOHN F. LEWIS.

DIRECTORS

Until March 31, 1897.	Until March 31, 1896.	Until March 31, 1895.
CHAS E MATHER,	SAML. T. KERR,	DAVID S. STETSON,
EDWIN S. CRAMP,	J. N. WALLEM,	S. B. MacDONNELL,
F. A. Von BOYNEBURGK,	J. S. W. HOLTON,	FRANK L. NEALL,
JOSIAH MONROE,	GEO. H. HIGBEE,	THOMAS WINSMORE,
JOSEPH A. BALL,	L. V. SCHERMERHORN,	GEO. E. EARNSHAW,
GEO. HARRISS, JR.	CHAS. F. GILLER,	F. A. CHURCHMAN,
	JOHN H. THOMPSON.	

COMMITTEES

Finance.	*Floor and Library.*	*Membership.*
JOSIAH MONROE,	J. S. W. HOLTON,	CHAS. E. MATHER,
JOHN H. THOMPSON,	SAML. T. KERR,	J. N. WALLEM,
JOSEPH A. BALL.	GEO. HARRISS, JR.	F. A. Von BOYNEBURGK.

Harbor, Pilotage and Station.	*Commerce and Transportation.*	*Executive.*
FRANK L. NEALL,	THOMAS WINSMORE,	GEO. E. EARNSHAW,
DAVID S. STETSON,	S. B. MacDONNELL,	THOMAS WINSMORE,
EDWIN S. CRAMP,	F. A. CHURCHMAN,	FRANK L. NEALL,
J. S. W. HOLTON,	GEO. H. HIGBEE,	J. S. W. HOLTON,
L. V. SCHERMERHORN.	CHAS. F. GILLER.	CHAS. E. MATHER,
		JOSIAH MONROE.

The rooms of The Philadelphia Maritime Exchange are located in the old Merchants' Exchange Building, at Walnut, Third and Dock streets, within a short distance of the Delaware River and in the heart of the commercial district of the city. This building was once the great rallying place of the solid business men of the city, and even in this day of colossal architecture has few superiors in the beauty of its design.

The Philadelphia Maritime Exchange quarters occupy the greater portion of the second floor, including the office of the Secretary; upon the floor above a well-furnished committee room is maintained. Strangers in the city desiring to visit the rooms are always made welcome. The staff of the Philadelphia Maritime Exchange is as follows:

E. R. SHARWOOD, *Secretary.* JAMES T. KERNAN, *Telephone Attendant.*
ELISHA CROWELL, *Assistant Secretary.* FRANK A. CAREY, *Messenger.*
CLARENCE N LUTZ, *Chief Clerk.* WILLIAM BOYER, *Messenger.*
JOHN H. WILLAR, *Marine Reporter.* THOMAS S. HARRIS, *Usher.*
FRANK W. SHOEMAKER, *Stenographer.*

The following Floor Regulations of The Maritime Exchange will be found interesting to ship owners, captains, and business men identified with our Merchant Marine:

Cards of Admission.

Upon each Certificate of Membership one card of admission shall be issued by the Secretary, which shall entitle the member to admission to the rooms of the Exchange, and privileges and benefits thereof; but corporations and firms shall designate one person in whose name the card of admission is to be issued; such person shall be an officer of the corporation, or a member of the firm designating him and shall become thereby the duly accredited representative thereof, and entitled to vote for it at the meetings of the Exchange, and be subject in all respects to the By-Laws and Rules and Regulations.

Cards of admission must be shown at the door upon request.

Pilots' Tickets.

If the manager of any Pennsylvania or Delaware pilot boat is an active member of the Exchange in good standing, cards of admission may be issued, at the discretion of the Floor and Library Committee, to every other pilot attached to the same boat. Such cards shall state the name of the pilot and of the boat to which he is attached, and shall become void if he ceases to be attached to that boat.

Shipmasters' Tickets.

Cards of admission to the floor, good for ten days, may be issued at discretion of the Floor and Library Committee, to masters in actual command of vessels in service.

Visitors' Tickets.

Non-resident visitors to the Exchange must be introduced by a member in good standing, and their names shall be registered in a book provided for that purpose. A visitor so introduced may receive a card of admission good for six consecutive days, and the same can be renewed at discretion of the Floor and Library Committee. Should such visitor violate the By-Laws or Regulations by the transaction of business on the floor, or in any other manner whatsoever, the member introducing him shall be held responsible for such violation.

Unauthorized use of Tickets.

The door-keeper shall take up any card of admission presented by a person not authorized under the By-Laws or Regulations of the Exchange to use the same, and shall refuse admission to such person.

Temporary Tickets.

A temporary card of admission, good until the day of the next succeeding regular meeting of the Board of Directors, may be issued at the discretion of the Floor and Library Committee, upon the recommendation of the Membership Committee, to any candidate for membership.

Substitute Tickets.

During the temporary absence of a member from the city, or during his illness confining him to his house, a substitute card of admission, good for not exceeding thirty days, may be issued at the discretion of the Floor and Library Committee, upon written request therefor.

The same right shall be enjoyed by the duly accredited representative of a corporation or firm.

Complimentary Tickets.

Complimentary cards of admission may be issued as authorized by the Board of Directors from time to time; such cards to be signed by the President and attested by the Secretary.

Lost Tickets.

Duplicates may be issued in place of lost cards of admission by the same authority and in the same manner that the originals were granted.

Special Service.

Telephone and Messenger Service.

All maritime information in possession of the main office of the Exchange can be obtained by any member promptly and without charge, on application personally at the rooms, or by telephone, messenger or letter. For example, if a member wishes to know the position of a certain vessel, he is entitled to and will receive at once all the information in possession of the office at the time inquiry is made.

On the other hand, if a member requests in advance that he shall be kept advised either by telephone, messenger, or letter, of all movements or information in regard to a particular vessel, or vessels, or cargoes, such request involves extra service, which must be paid for at special rates.

Rates.

Single request in advance for telephone, messenger, or letter report, of the sailing, arrival, or passing a reporting point, or any one item of information in regard to any particular vessel or cargo, ten cents, payable when request therefor is made, or monthly, or as may be arranged for by the Floor and Library Committee.

Special service by telephone, messenger or letter, of the sailing, arrival or passing a reporting point, of a particular line of vessels, or a particular ownership, or a number of vessels, or the continued movements of a single vessel, can be arranged for with the Floor and Library Committee.

Direct News from Stations.

Superintendents of Reporting Stations and of the Lewes Branch Office are instructed to answer inquiries received direct from members, as to questions of fact within their own knowledge, such answers to be sent through the Exchange when practicable. A charge of fifty cents will be made for each answer, exclusive of telegraph tolls, if any.

Business Hours.

The business hours of the Exchange shall be as follows:

Week-days (Saturdays excepted), from 8 A. M. until 6 P. M.

Saturdays, from 8 A. M. until 4 P. M., except between June 15th and September 15th, when the Exchange will close at noon.

Legal holidays, from 9 to 10 A. M.

All of which are subject to the discretion of the Floor and Library Committee.

Records and Bulletins on File in The Maritime Exchange.

CONGRESSIONAL AND STATE LEGISLATIVE RECORDS.

DELAWARE BAY AND RIVER NEWS.—Embracing the movements of all classes of vessels as observed from the stations of the Exchange in the Bay and River Delaware.

ARRIVALS—FOREIGN AND COASTWISE.—Comprising all arrivals of vessels at Philadelphia from foreign and coastwise ports.

CLEARANCES—FOREIGN AND COASTWISE.—Comprising all clearances of vessels from Philadelphia to foreign and coastwise ports.

IMPORTS.—A complete record of manifests of cargoes of all vessels from foreign ports.

EXPORTS.—A complete record of all manifests of cargoes of vessels leaving Philadelphia for foreign ports.

FOREIGN CABLE SHIPPING NEWS.—The movements of vessels in the American trade at foreign ports, as received by cable.

DOMESTIC SHIPPING NEWS.—The movements of vessels at American ports, other than Philadelphia.

DISASTERS AND MISCELLANEOUS.—The earliest intelligence procurable respecting disasters, detentions and maritime items of general interest, from all parts of the world.

CHARTER BOOK.—Record of charters made at and from American ports.

MAIL STEAMERS.—The names of steamers and hour for closing outward mails at Philadelphia and New York; the hour of sighting inward mail steamers, with the time their mails will be ready for delivery; changes, detentions, etc.

FINANCIAL REPORTS.—Daily quotations of exchange in European monetary centres, the fluctuations of bonds, stocks, consols, rentes, etc., on the London Stock Exchange and Paris Bourse, embracing "Governments" and general securities, silver quotations, Paris Exchange on London, specie statements of the Bank of England, Bank of France and the Imperial Bank of Germany, with their current rates of discount; also, similar intelligence from the principal monetary centres of the United States, including fluctuations in the principal bonds, railroad stocks and mining securities, notice of dividends declared, and Clearing House statements from Boston to San Francisco.

MARKET REPORTS.—Embracing the quotations for the day in all the principal trade centres of grain, petroleum, cotton, provisions, and, in fact, all staples for both immediate and future delivery; together with the tone and special features of the markets and rates of freight by rail, steam and sail, both inland and ocean.

CABLE QUOTATIONS from the principal cities of England, France, Germany and other European markets for grain, petroleum, provisions, cotton, coffee, etc., in detail; also, foreign specialties and freight in various directions, the coffee market at Rio Janeiro and Cuba sugar market.

STATISTICS relating to the export and import trade of the United States.

DISTINGUISHING DAY MARKS AND NIGHT SIGNALS of the different steamship lines.

LIGHT-HOUSE NOTICES, with the latest changes in lights, buoys, etc.

CONSULAR REPORTS from abroad to the Government at Washington.

WEATHER REPORT OF THE UNITED STATES WEATHER BUREAU.—This is received daily, at about 10.30 A. M. It consists of a detailed statement of the barometer, thermometer, direction and velocity of the wind, and other phenomena as observed at 7. A. M., 75th meridian time, at about eighty stations of the Signal Service. This data is entered on an outline map of the United States, and isobare and isothermal lines are drawn, showing at a glance the meteorological conditions of the whole country. The weather indications of the twenty-four hours commencing at 3 P. M. of the day on which the map is posted, are also given. A Coast Bulletin is prepared daily at the Exchange, showing the direction and velocity of the wind and the state of the weather at eighteen stations on the Atlantic Coast, from Eastport, Maine, to Key West, Florida, and including the principal Ports in the Gulf of Mexico. In addition to the regular reports, special bulletins received at the United States Weather Bureau in this city are promptly posted. These include Cold Wave warnings, Frost warnings, movements of approaching storms, and other items of interest.

HYDROGRAPHIC OFFICE.—The United States Branch Hydrographic Office, under the charge of an officer of the Navy, is located at the Exchange rooms, affording masters of vessels free information in a practical form.

GENERAL NEWS.—Embracing items of miscellaneous character, such as Business Failures, Fires, Quarantine and other official notices; important legal decisions in Admiralty, and Press dispatches from all parts of the world.

LIST OF VESSELS IN PORT.—Showing Nationality, rig, tonnage, location, employment, name of master and agent.

LOGS.—Abstracts from logs of incoming steamers, showing the character of the weather, etc., experienced during the voyage.

COMMERCIAL CIRCULARS in great variety, from the principal ports of the world, domestic and foreign, showing the actual state of trade in detail, by latest mail advices.

CODE BOOKS.—Watkins, Scott, A 1, Commercial, A. B. C., and Hunter & Patten.

BOOKS OF REFERENCE.—Century Dictionary, Webster's Unabridged Dictionary, Atlases (foreign and domestic), London Post Office Directory, Directories of Principal American Cities, United States Revised Statutes, Laws of Pennsylvania, Ordinances of City of Philadelphia, Shipping Records (American and foreign), Port Charges of the World, Gazetteer of the World, Congressional Record, Philadelphia and New York Securities, Reports of United States Engineers on the Harbors of the United States, Navigation Laws of the United States, Customs Regulations of the United States, Reports of Maritime and Commercial Bodies, and an extensive Library of other Commercial Works of Reference.

Tide Table for the Port of Philadelphia and Delaware River and Bay.

Showing the difference between the time of High Water at Philadelphia (Walnut Street Wharf, Delaware River) and the following places.

The hours and minutes standing against the place in this table are to be added or subtracted from the time of High Water at Philadelphia on any given day, which will give (nearly) the time of High Water at the following points:

(+ signifies ADD; — signifies SUBTRACT.)

DISTANCES.	Distance from Walnut Street Wharf, Philadelphia, in *Nautical Miles*, to the following Places, and the Difference in Time of High Water at Each Point.	DIFFERENCE IN TIME. H. M.
2½ miles.	Port Richmond Elevator, Philadelphia...................	+ .08
¾ "	Cooper's Point, New Jersey...........................	+ .11
0 "	Walnut Street Wharf, Philadelphia.....................	
1⅜ "	Kaighn's Point, New Jersey...........................	— .10
3⅛ "	Greenwich Point, Philadelphia.........................	— .18
7 "	Girard Point, (Schuylkill River).......................	— .30
9¼ "	Point Breeze Oil Works (Schuylkill River)...............	— .35
9½ "	Gibson's Point (Schuylkill River)......................	— .37
12⅜ "	Chestnut St. Wharf (Schuylkill River)..................	— .40
11½ "	Pennsylvania State Quarantine Station.................	— .45
14¼ "	Chester, Pennsylvania................................	— .57
15⅝ "	Schooner Ledge, Delaware River......................	—1.05
17¾ "	**Marcus Hook Reporting Station**.....................	—1.14
23⅝ "	Cherry Island Flats, Delaware River...................	—1.40
24¾ "	Wilmington, Delaware (mouth of Christiana Creek).......	—1.45
26 "	Deep Water Point, New Jersey........................	—1.42
29¼ "	**New Castle Reporting Station**......................	—1.51
33⅝ "	Fort Delaware..	—2.02
38¼ "	**Reedy Island Reporting Station**....................	—2.14
44⅝ "	Liston's Point..	—3.15
48 "	Bombay Hook..	—3.27
65½ "	Cross Ledge Lighthouse..............................	—4.40
77⅝ "	Brandywine Lighthouse...............................	—5.37
82½ "	Cape May...	—5.20
89 "	**Delaware Breakwater Reporting Station**..............	—5.42
111¾ "	Five Fathom Bank Lightship..........................	
11¼ "	N. N. E. ⅜ E. Magnetic from the Five Fathom Bank Lightship is located the Northeast End Lightship................	

AVERAGE DURATION OF TIDES.

	RISE. h. m.	FALL. h. m.
Philadelphia...	5.06	7.19
New Castle...	5.24	7.01
Delaware Breakwater....................................	6.17	6.08

	SPRING TIDES.	NEAP TIDES.	AVERAGE TIDES.
At Philadelphia..............	6.2 feet.	4.5 feet.	5.4 feet.
At New Castle	6.9 "	4.4 "	5.7 "
At Delaware Breakwater.	4.5 "	3.0 "	3.5 "

Compass Variation at Philadelphia, 6° Westerly.

Brief Outline of the Work of the Philadelphia Maritime Exchange since its Organization, in 1875.

COMPILED BY THE SECRETARY.

—1875—

Demurrage and Lay-day Scale for grain and pretroleum vessels adopted.
Charter-parties for grain, fruit, and coal adopted.

—1876—

Congress memorialized regarding a bill (H. R. 654) to amend the United States Shipping Act of June, 1872.

Congress memorialized to pass the "Hale Bill" to repeal compulsory pilotage on coastwise vessels.

Congress petitioned to make an appropriation for the United States Hydrographic Office.

—1877—

The petition of the Board of Wardens for the extension of the Warden's line endorsed.

Resolutions adopted relative to the presentation and collection of claims growing out of the Pittsburg riots.

Resolutions adopted commending the appointment of Hon. John Welsh as United States Minister to the Court of St. James.

—1878—

Special Committee appointed to urge upon Congress the need of an appropriation for the improvement of the Delaware Harbor and River.

Resolutions adopted opposing the transfer of the United States Life-Saving Service from the Treasury to the Navy Department.

An improvement in the Postal facilities between Philadelphia and Lewes, Del., advocated.

The removal of the United States Signal Station from Lewes, Del., to Delaware Breakwater suggested.

The proposed abolition by City Councils of the Board of Wardens for the Port of Philadelphia opposed.

—1879—

Resolutions forwarded to City Councils suggesting the presentation by the commercial bodies of Philadelphia of the names of gentlemen qualified to fulfil the duties of Port Wardens.

Congress memorialized to appropriate $5,000 to establish a Signal Station on the Delaware Breakwater.

MAP OF THE DELAWARE RIVER, BELOW PHILADELPHIA.

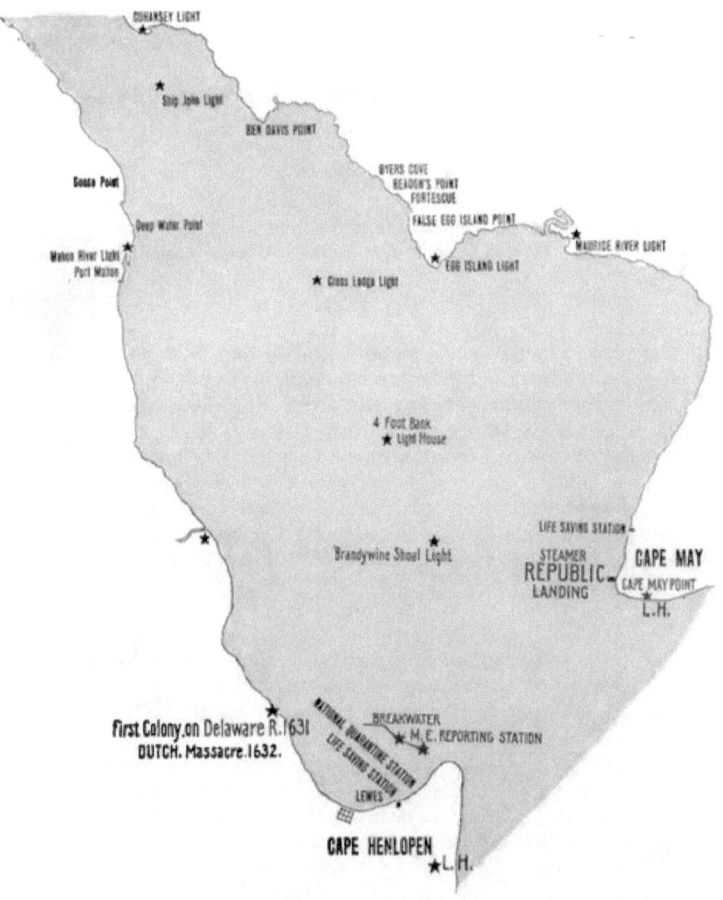

MAP OF DELAWARE BAY.

Congress memorialized in favor of the passage of Senate Bill, 1561, providing for the interchange of subsidiary silver coins and United States notes.

Bankruptcy Bill prepared by the Philadelphia Board of Trade, endorsed by the Exchange.

Physical examination of seamen before shipment, as suggested by the Secretary of the Treasury and the Surgeon-General of the Marine Hospital Service, approved.

Delegation sent to Washington to favor an appropriation for the improvement of the Delaware and Schuylkill Rivers.

—1880—

Congress memorialized in opposition to the law requiring the payment of three months' extra wages to seamen discharged in foreign ports.

Resolutions adopted opposing any division of the Organization of the United States Signal Service.

Resolutions adopted favoring an annual appropriation by Councils of a sufficient amount of money necessary to maintain a proper depth of water in the docks along the river front to accommodate large vessels.

Delegation appointed to attend Shipping Convention at Boston.

Building and equipment of Reporting Station at Cape Henlopen.

—1881—

Resolutions adopted favoring the discontinuance of "Spout Service" charges at Girard Point Elevators.

Delegation sent to Harrisburg on "Pilotage Reform."

Defining the limits of the Port of Philadelphia.

Resolutions adopted commending the services of Commodore Geo. B. White, U. S. N., while Inspector of the Fourth Light-house District.

Resolutions adopted on the death of President Garfield.

Resolutions adopted favoring National legislation to correct abuses arising from the payment of advance wages to seamen.

"Protective Fund" for vessels inaugurated.

Resolutions adopted in testimony of the continued and increasing usefulness of the Signal Service of the United States.

Action by the Exchange relative to the infringement of regulations by reason of vessels anchoring within the range of the "Range Lights."

Change made in the "Lay-day Scale" for vessels loading petroleum, to conform to the charges enforced at the Port of New York.

Resolutions favoring the principles of differential rates of freight, founded upon the difference in the service rendered to and from the west and the cities of New York, Philadelphia and Baltimore.

—1882—

Resolutions adopted favoring the introduction by the Government of the "Pintsch" system of lighting buoys for use on the coast and navigable waters.

Resolutions adopted favoring the early completion of the new Post Office Building at Philadelphia.

Delegation sent to Washington to urge the claims of the Port of Philadelphia for a liberal appropriation for the improvement of the Delaware River and Bay.

Committee appointed to prepare a paper, to be submitted to the United States Advisory Commission appointed to hear arguments upon differential rates of freight from the west to the seaboard.

Congress memorialized in favor of the permanent organization of the United States Signal Service.

Resolutions adopted in opposition to the proposed bridge across the Delaware between Philadelphia and Camden, N. J.

Exchange incorporated.

Resolutions adopted protesting against the extension of the patents to the inventors of "Steam Grain Shovels."

Bi-centennial Anniversary of the Commonwealth of Pennsylvania endorsed.

Resolutions adopted favoring the passage of the bill reported by Senator Frye for the disposition of the French Spoliation Claims.

Endorsement of the Master Stevedores' Protective Association of the Port of Philadelphia.

Committee appointed to co-operate with a committee of the New York Maritime Association in an inquiry into the causes of the decline in American shipping.

—1883—

Congress memorialized in favor of the retention of the United States Shipping Commissioner's Office.

Congress memorialized in opposition to the proposed transfer of the United States Coast and Geodetic Survey, the United States Revenue Marine, the United States Marine Hospital Service and the United States Signal Service from the Departments they are now connected with.

Congress memorialized in favor of the establishment of a Light-ship off the Capes of Virginia.

Congress memorialized in favor of the reduction of the duty on molasses to the same ratio as that upon the lower grades of sugar.

Memorial sent to the Committee on Commerce of the House of Representatives at Washington, urging the appropriation of $50,000 from the River and Harbor Appropriation for the improvement of the Delaware River in the vicinity of Petty's Island.

United States Senate Committee on Commerce memorialized in favor of the passage of the measure known as the "Dingley" Shipping Bill. (H. R. 7061.)

Legislature of the State of Pennsylvania memorialized in favor of the passage of a bill looking to the improvement of the stevedore service at the Port of Philadelphia.

Committee appointed to act with a committee of the Tow Boat Owners' Association as a joint Arbitration Committee.

Finance Committee of Councils memorialized to appropriate the sum of $10,000 for the purpose of dredging the docks into which the city sewers empty.

Committee appointed to co-operate with other commercial bodies in asking Congress to make liberal appropriations for the improvement of the Delaware River and Bay.

Committee appointed on improvement of American shipping.

—1884—

Delegates appointed to attend "Bankruptcy Bill" Convention at Washington.

Resolutions adopted favoring the application, by the Schuylkill River East Side Railroad Company, to the Board of Wardens for the Port of Philadelphia, for a license to erect a bridge across the Schuylkill River.

Resolutions adopted favoring an appropriation by Congress for the supply to American Consuls, in foreign ports, of copies of "Port Charges of the World."

Resolutions adopted favoring the establishment on a firm basis of the United States Hydrographic Office, and an appropriation for the continuance of Branch Hydrographic Offices at the principal seaboard cities of the United States.

Resolutions adopted urging the Pennsylvania delegates in Congress to support the "Dingley Pilotage Bill."

Rates of wharfage at petroleum wharves approved by the Exchange.

—1885—

Appropriations urged at Washington for the improvement of the Delaware River and Bay.

Resolutions adopted endorsing the application of the New York Maritime Association, and others, for the establishment of an United States Marine Hospital at the Port of New York.

Delegates appointed to a Joint Committee of Commercial Bodies for the purpose of formulating an International Bill of Lading.

Committee appointed to urge upon the Legislature of the State of Pennsylvania the passage of a bill having for its purpose the correction of discriminations in freight rates by Railroad Companies.

City Councils memorialized in favor of an appropriation for the establishment of a Nautical Schoolship at Philadelphia.

—1886—

Resolution adopted favoring the establishment by the United States Signal Service of a Signal and Reporting Station at Jupiter Inlet, Florida.

Resolution adopted protesting against the reduction of the duty on sugars 20 per cent., and leaving the duty on molasses as at present, as contemplated in the Morrison Tariff Bill (H. R. 5576).

Congress memorialized in connection with the testing of anchors and chains of vessels.

Resolutions adopted favoring an appeal to the public for contributions in behalf of the families of members of the Barnegat, N. J., Life-Saving Crew, who lost their lives in the line of duty on February 11, 1886.

The "Lowell" Bankruptcy Bill, as amended by the United States Senate, endorsed.

Resolutions adopted favoring the abrogation by Congress of the Hawaiian Reciprocity Treaty.

Congress memorialized to appoint a Commission to suggest amendments to the Navigation Laws, more particularly relating to passenger vessels.

—1887—

Committee appointed to attend Shipping Convention at Washington.

Congress memorialized to appropriate $25,000 for the purpose of making a preliminary survey to determine the feasibility of removing Smith and Windmill Islands.

"Maritime Rules" for the Port of Philadelphia adopted.

Legislature of Pennsylvania memorialized in opposition to House Bill No. 6, relating to the erection of wharves and the collection of wharfage thereon, unless a proviso be attached preventing interference with the powers of the Board of Wardens of Philadelphia, in their supervision of wharves and piers in the Delaware.

"Strike Clause" adopted for insertion in "Maritime Rules" for the Port of Philadelphia.

Board of Wardens memorialized to withhold their sanction to pilots taking upon their boats any more apprentices until the number of pilots already licensed more nearly approaches the requirements of commerce.

President of the United States memorialized in favor of an International Marine Conference.

—1888—

Congress memorialized to establish a permanent light on Swan Point Bar, Chesapeake Bay.

Resolutions adopted protesting against a proposed unjust discrimination in the Mills Tariff Bill (H. R. 9051) as being injurious to Philadelphia industries and its maritime interests.

Congress memorialized in favor of an appropriation for the maintenance of Branch Hydrographic offices.

Resolutions adopted endorsing the efforts of the Philadelphia members of Congress to obtain recognition from Congress for the permanent improvement of the League Island Navy Yard.

Resolutions adopted welcoming the proposed elevated branch of the Philadelphia & Reading Railroad into the city.

—1889—

Congress memorialized in favor of the establishment of a Naval Reserve.

Congress memorialized in favor of the passage of a bill (S. 2851) to amend the Interstate Commerce Act.

Resolutions adopted favoring the passage of an Ordinance by City Councils granting to the Philadelphia & Reading Railroad Co. the terminal privileges desired, under proper and just restrictions.

Resolutions adopted advocating the establishment of a Belt Line Railroad.

Resolutions adopted in opposition to House bill No. 52, known as the "Grade Crossing" Bill.

Committee appointed to solicit subscriptions for the families of pilots lost with the pilot boat "Enoch Turley."

Committee appointed to solicit subscriptions in money, etc., in aid of those left destitute by the Johnstown floods.

Resolutions adopted commending the services of the employés of the Maritime Exchange and of the Light-Houses on the Delaware Breakwater in connection with the rescue of the Captain and crew of the Norwegian Bark "Patriot," wrecked at that point May 23, 1889.

Resolutions adopted looking to the removal by the Government of wrecked coal barges sunk in the Delaware Bay, in positions dangerous to navigation, during the storm of September 3 to 12, 1889.

City Councils memorialized to appropriate $200,000 for acquiring the title to the islands in the Delaware River opposite the City of Philadelphia.

Congress memorialized in favor of the proposed transfer of the United States Revenue Marine Service from the Treasury to the Navy Department, as recited in the Chandler Bill (S. 3924).

—1890—

Delegate appointed to attend the convention of the Industrial Shipping League at Washington.

"Torrey" Bankruptcy Bill endorsed.

Congress Memorialized to establish a Department of Commerce.

Congress memorialized to appoint a Board of Engineers to examine and report upon a National Harbor of Refuge near the mouth of the Delaware Bay, suitable for deep draught vessels.

Congress memorialized in favor of the payment of a pension to the widow of the late Commodore George B. White, U. S. N.

Congress memorialized in favor of an appropriation for a new light-ship on Fenwicks Island Shoal, and the retention of the light-ship at present on that shoal as a Relief light-vessel for the Fourth Light-house District.

Report of the American Delegates to the International Marine Conference endorsed.

A proposed proportionate increase in the rates of wharfage on vessels loading petroleum at Philadelphia endorsed.

Secretary of the Treasury memorialized in favor of an increase in the number of weighers and gaugers at Philadelphia.

Committee appointed to urge upon Congress a liberal appropriation for the improvement of the Schuylkill River.

Committee appointed to urge upon Congress an appropriation of $50,000 for the reopening of the League Island Navy Yard.

Memorial resolutions adopted on the death of Mr. William Brockie, late President of the Exchange.

Congress memorialized to pass a Joint Resolution, requiring the several Departments of the Government to examine and report upon the recommendations of the American Delegates to the International Marine Conference, with a view to obtaining legislation thereon.

—1891—

Protest forwarded to Congress against the passage of the Free Silver Coinage Bill.

The Legislature of Pennsylvania memorialized against the removal of the Quarantine Station from its present location at the Lazaretto.

Committee appointed to represent the Exchange on a Joint Committee of Commercial Bodies, to consider all matters relating to the improvement of the Harbor of Philadelphia.

Legislature of Pennsylvania memorialized against the passage of the Direct Tax Bill (H. R. 210).

Delegation sent to Harrisburg to protest against the passage of the Bill providing for the removal of the Quarantine Station from the Lazaretto.

United States Engineers petitioned to dredge a cut through Bulkhead Shoals, to allow the passage of deep draught vessels.

Action of Exchange in inducing Masters of Line Steamers to accept the first Pilot offering his services.

Charges adopted regulating the discharge of sugar cargoes at the Port of Philadelphia.

Minute adopted relative to the death of Mr. William G. Boulton, late Vice-President of the Exchange.

Prizes awarded by the Exchange to the graduates of the Pennsylvania Nautical Schoolship "Saratoga."

Resolutions adopted favoring the transfer of the United States Revenue Marine Service from the Treasury to the Navy Department.

—1892—

Congress memorialized in opposition to the measure establishing Load Lines for vessels (S. 1226).

Resolutions adopted favoring an increase in the present Steamship Service facilities between Philadelphia and Savannah.

Congress memorialized in favor of a bill (S. 3017) providing for a new Revenue Boarding Cutter for the Port of Philadelphia.

Committee appointed to confer with the Board of Health relative to unnecessary detention of vessels in quarantine.

Resolutions adopted expressive of the appreciation of the Exchange of the labor of Mr. Spencer C. McCorkel, Assistant to the United States Coast and Geodetic Survey stationed at Philadelphia, and regret at his retirement.

Committee appointed to represent the Exchange on a joint committee for the consideration of the subject of a Philadelphia Transportation Bureau.

Committee appointed to co-operate with the local United States Engineer in an endeavor to put a stop to the practice of dumping mud in the channels of the Delaware River, as being detrimental to the best interests of the Port.

Arrangements made with the General Superintendent of the Life-Saving Service at Washington to connect the telephone lines of the Life-Saving Service between Cape Henlopen and Cape Charles, with the Branch Office of the Exchange at Lewes, Del.

City Councils memorialized in favor of the establishment on Little Tinicum Island of a temporary disinfecting plant.

Resolutions adopted favoring a National Quarantine Law.

—1893—

Congress memorialized to pass a law to legalize and make effective the provisions of the "New York Produce Exchange Bill of Lading."

Congress memorialized in favor of the construction and early completion of the Nicaragua Canal.

Minute adopted relative to the death of Mr. Lars. Westergaard, late Treasurer of the Exchange.

Resolutions adopted commending the work done by the City Ice Boats.

Committee appointed to consider "Load Line" Rules adopted by the British Board of Trade.

Delegation sent to Harrisburg to favor the passage of the "Bliss" Quarantine Bill.

Secretary of the Treasury addressed relative to the vessels loading at Marcus Hook Oil Piers being required to clear from the Wilmington Custom House instead of from Philadelphia, as heretofore.

Ocean Steamship Bill of Lading adopted by the Exchange.

Grain Charter-parties (steam) "direct port" and "for orders" adopted by the Exchange.

Congress memorialized in favor of the passage of a Joint Resolution authorizing the President of the United States to make with other governments an International Agreement providing for the reporting, marking, and removal of dangerous wrecks, derelicts, and other menaces to navigation in the North Atlantic Ocean.

Resolutions adopted favoring the passage of a law by Congress:

First.—Requiring the Navy Department to remove or destroy wrecks that are not salvable.

Second.—Defining mode of procedure in reporting, marking and removing wrecks and derelicts.

Third.—Providing for the construction, equipment, and maintenance on the Atlantic Coast, and waters bordering thereon, of one or more seagoing steamers, specially adapted for removing and destroying wrecks and derelicts.

Fourth.—Requiring the Light-House Board to mark and light wrecks and obstructions.

Fifth.—Amending the Act of September 19, 1890, so as to authorize the War Department to remove obstructions in a shorter period than two months.

Consideration by the Board of the subject of "heat and light" on board vessels loading petroleum at oil wharves in the Port of Philadelphia.

Proposed change by the Light-House Board in the character of lights at present displayed at the mouth of the Christiana River, Delaware, approved.

An oil painting of the late Mr. William Brockie, first president of the Maritime Exchange, placed in the Exchange rooms by subscription of members.

Cable laid at Reedy Island, connecting the Quaratine Station at that point with Philadelphia by telegraph.

The Government of the Netherlands, through the Minister at Washington, requested by the Exchange to establish a Vice-Consulate at Philadelphia.

Spanish Consul at Philadelphia communicated with, relative to the different conditions under which "Certificates of Origin" are issued at this port, as compared with other ports.

Congress memorialized to enact Senate Bill 869, and Bill H. R. 2795, providing for the maintenance in active service of Life-saving Stations upon the sea and gulf coasts of the United States for ten months in the year.

President of the United States memorialized to make prompt use of the powers conferred upon him by the Joint Resolution of Congress, authorizing him to make an International Agreement providing for the marking, reporting and removal of wrecks and derelicts.

An agent of the Exchange established at the National Quarantine Station at Reedy Island, as a Marine observer and telegraph operator.

Secretary of War memorialized in favor of the early completion of the work of filling in the Gap-Way between Delaware Breakwater proper and the Ice Breaker.

—1894—

Congress memorialized in favor of the passage of Bill H. R. 4606, modifying the penalty for the crime of Barratry.

Proposed publication by the United States Hydrographic Office of a pilot chart of the North Pacific Ocean commended as an important additional aid to navigation.

Resolutions adopted favoring the passage of the Bill S. 1435 (an amendment to Section 2880 of the Revised Statutes), fixing the time allowed for vessels to unlade.

Revision of the By-Laws and Floor Regulations of the Exchange.

Delegation sent to Washington to urge an appropriation by Congress for completing the closing of the Gap-Way at the Delaware Breakwater, and for the further improvement of the Schuylkill River.

Congress memorialized to make a liberal appropriation for the continuance of the work in connection with the improvement of the Delaware River.

Minute adopted relative to the death of Mr. George W. Childs.

Congress memorialized in favor of the early completion of the Sandy Bay Breakwater and Harbor of Refuge, at Cape Ann, Mass.

Congress memorialized to amend the bill under consideration relating to the employment of engineers, etc., on steam vessels, so that it shall not apply to vessels of 150 tons and under.

Congress memorialized in favor of the prompt construction of the Nicaragua Canal under American control.

Minute adopted relative to the death of Mr. Spencer C. McCorkle, Assistant United States Coast and Geodetic Survey.

Congress memorialized against the passage of certain bills introduced to amend the Navigation Laws, to-wit: H. R. 5501, 5502, 5503, 5504, 5505, 5506, and 5603, known as the "Maguire" Bills.

Committee appointed to prepare and issue a "Hand-Book of the Lower Delaware," of which a special feature shall be a description of the National Quarantine Stations at Delaware Breakwater and Reedy Island.

Gas-lighted Buoy placed on the "Elbow of Cross Ledge," Delaware River, at the solicitation of the Exchange.

Congress memorialized in favor of the retention of the United States Coast and Geodetic Survey in the Treasury Department.

Communication addressed to the Superintendent of the United States Coast and Geodetic Survey at Washington, calling his attention to the filling up of the Harbor of the Delaware Breakwater, and asking that a survey be made of that harbor at as early a date as possible. [Note.—Survey made November, 1894.]

Collector of Customs at Philadelphia advised as to the nature and extent of taxes imposed on shipping in Ports of the United States, in answer to an inquiry made by him.

President of the Exchange appeared before the Committee on Merchant Marine and Fisheries of the House of Representatives, at Washington, in company with representatives from the Maritime Association of the Port of New York, in opposition to bills amending the Navigation Laws, introduced by Mr. Maguire, of California.

Congress memorialized against the passage of Bill H. R. 7295, prohibiting the payment of advance wages to seamen.

City Councils memorialized to appropriate $500,000 for the improvement of the Delaware and Schuylkill Rivers.

Light-House Board petitioned to replace the Nun Buoy at Dan Baker with a Gas Buoy.

Committee appointed to consider the subject of "Quarantine" on the Delaware River and Bay.

Secretary of the Treasury petitioned to have established and maintained at the National Quarantine Station, Reedy Island, a tidal indicator, to advise vessels of the depth of water over "Dan Baker Shoals" and "Duck Creek Flats."

Tidal gauges ordered by the Exchange to be located at points on the Delaware River, to aid vessels in passing over the shoals at "Fort Mifflin," "Schooner Ledge," "Cherry Island," and "Bulkhead."

—1895—

(TO FEBRUARY 25TH.)

Senators from Pennsylvania urged to have inserted in the Sundry Civil Bill an item for an appropriation for a light-vessel to be placed on "Overfalls Shoals," entrance to Delaware Bay.

Governor of Pennsylvania memorialized to require familiarity with shipping, experience, energy, and tact as special qualifications in his appointee for Harbor Master of the Port of Philadelphia.

Committee appointed to urge upon the Legislature of Pennsylvania the need of an appropriation by the State for the improvement of the Delaware and Schuylkill Rivers.

President of the United States memorialized in favor of Consular Reform.

Senate of the United States memorialized against the passage of Bill (H. R. 4609) known as the "Bailey" Bankruptcy Bill, and in favor of the "Torrey" Bill.

Committee appointed to recommend to the Secretary of the Treasury suitable bearings or ranges to define the lines dividing the high seas from rivers, harbors and inland waters.

LIGHT-HOUSE AND MARITIME EXCHANGE REPORTING STATION, BREAKWATER.

The Philadelphia Maritime Exchange Reporting Stations.

One of the most important functions of The Philadelphia Maritime Exchange is the telegraphic reporting of incoming and outgoing vessels from its chain of stations along the river and bay. These reporting stations are located at Delaware Breakwater, Lewes, Del., Reedy Island (National quarantine station), New Castle, Del., and Marcus Hook, Pa. The lower station upon the storm-beaten Breakwater is connected with the mainland by a telegraph cable, which, from its frequent breakage by vessels anchoring in its vicinity, is one of the largest items of expense connected with this invaluable service. In addition to the instantaneous reporting and bulletining of all vessels, communication by telephone is maintained at the branch office, at Lewes, Del., with all of the near-by life saving stations, and all wrecks or other marine casualties are promptly reported for the public information.

The lower Reporting Station is a weather-stained but staunch little building upon the western end of the Breakwater. The Breakwater itself is half a mile long, and rises about twelve feet above the sea level. It is simply a mass of rocks dumped into the sea by prodigious labor until the required rampart was completed. The survey of the work was commenced about 1825. Running at right angles with it, and at a distance of about 400 yards, is another stone pile. The intermediate gap is filled up to low water surface.

The signal station is a one-floor frame house, clamped and chained to heavy beams anchored into the rocks. Just beyond it is the tower of the "front" light of the Breakwater. At the eastern end of the Breakwater is another light. Boats hang from davits upon the exterior of the signal station, by which the three men on duty may in turn go to and from the shore. The station contains four rooms: the general room, in which are the telegraph instrument, signal flags, telescope, etc.; a kitchen, and two bed-rooms. Outside is the flagstaff, from which the signal flags flutter.

Every ship passing up the bay reports her name by means of the International Signal Code, and such other facts as may be of value or interest to her consignees or owners. By the same method orders are communicated to tugs. Storm and weather signals are also displayed. The worst storm ever known at the Breakwater occurred September 7 to 11, 1889, when thirty-two vessels were driven ashore, all of which, except seven, were afterwards floated. Occasionally a storm drives a ship upon the solid mass of the Breakwater, as in the case of the "Morro Castle," November 27, 1888, from which, happily, the entire crew were heroically rescued by the inmates of the signal station and the light-house. Another ship, the Norwegian bark "Patriot," was wrecked here in May, 1889, and again the crew were saved.

The population of the little town of Lewes finds occupation in the employ of the Government, the Maritime Exchange, and the wrecking concerns, piloting, and other business of the sea; and life in such a community, although in the main monotonous, is often punctuated by the most stirring excitements when, as in the case of great shipwrecks, such as are an inevitable part of seafaring enterprises, half drowned strangers are cast among them, the care of whom is accepted as a matter of course by the humblest cottager upon the sands. That Lewes has its memories and romances may be well imagined. Local tradition tells of British men-of-war that plagued its people in the Revolution and the War of 1812, and sent their shot through the gray little cabins. Here, during her early life, resided the famous litigant, Myra Clark Gaines, and Cæsar Rodney, one of the signers of the Declaration of Independence, lived here. In the cemetery of the Protestant Episcopal Church are the graves of many a staunch pilot, many a stranger whose life was ended by the waves upon this desolate coast.

Recently a survey has been made by Government engineers for a much larger breakwater, or National harbor of refuge, located at a greater distance from the shore, which when built will accommodate the largest modern vessels, and provide far greater safety by the increased sea room and depth of water than that now in existence.

The employés stationed at the Breakwater Reporting Station are: John H. Richards, Superintendent; W. A. Johnson, Assistant Superintendent and Boatman; Frank Fuss, Assistant and Telegraph Operator.

Upon the mainland, at Lewes, the Maritime Exchange has a branch station in charge of F. H. Brewer, Agent; Antoinette Brewer, Assistant; John T. Johnson, Messenger.

Reedy Island Reporting Station.

The building of the quarantine structures at Reedy Island afforded an opportunity for the Maritime Exchange to locate a Reporting Station forming a tower-like enclosure at the southern end of the Government structure, commanding a view of the approach from both up and down the river. This office is in charge of Harry Hehl, under the supervision of the officer in command.

New Castle, Delaware, Reporting Station.

The office at this point is located in a two-story building facing the principal wharf. It is in charge of Hugh Duffy, as agent.

MARITIME EXCHANGE REPORTING STATION AT NEW CASTLE.

Marcus Hook Reporting Station.

This station is placed above the outer end of the extensive oil shipping sheds of the Bear Creek Refining Company. It is in charge of George J. Carter, as superintendent.

An interchange of news with kindred institutions at other ports keeps members posted in all matters of interest, and disseminates the news from the stations as well as that gathered along the docks and wharves of the city by the Exchange reporters.

MARITIME EXCHANGE REPORTING STATION AT MARCUS HOOK.

Life-Saving Service at the Capes of the Delaware.

In response to a request from the Philadelphia Maritime Exchange, the Superintendent of the United States Life-Saving Service has supplied the following interesting information:

TREASURY DEPARTMENT,

OFFICE OF THE GENERAL SUPERINTENDENT,

LIFE-SAVING SERVICE.

WASHINGTON, D. C., November 24, 1894.

SIR: I transmit herewith, in the form of a tabular statement, the only information of the kind that it is practicable to give. From the nature of things, the number of lives the Service saves cannot be even approximately stated. It would not be true to say that all who escaped death from wrecked vessels, at which life-saving crews were present, were saved by the Service, or even that all who were brought ashore by the Station boats and apparatus would otherwise have perished, because history has shown that on most occasions of shipwreck, where life-saving crews have not been present, a greater or less number of the shipwrecked have escaped.

On the other hand, the number of persons brought ashore by the life-saving boats and apparatus does not by any means represent the full number of lives saved, because many are saved upon stranded vessels which are got off and floated by the life-saving crews.

LIFE-SAVING STATION, CAPE MAY.

Again, the service annually, by the danger signals of its patrolmen, warns off a great number of vessels running into danger of stranding, saving most of them from damage or total loss. There were 244 such instances last year, and for many years past the number has never been less than 200. How many persons are preserved from death by this means can, of course, never be told.

In view of these and other considerations, the reports of the Service do not undertake to say how many lives the Life-Saving Service saves. The number of persons on board the vessels that meet with misfortune within the field of Station operations is known, and the number of these who are lost from such vessels is also known. In making up the wreck statistics, therefore, these numbers are stated.

You will understand, also, that the Life-Saving Service does not claim to have saved all the property under the caption of "amount of property saved," in the table. It is a fact, however, that the service, directly and indirectly, saves a vast amount, much more than the cost of maintaining the service.   Respectfully yours,

S. J. KIMBALL,
General Superintendent.

NOTE—For the use of this and the illustrations of Cape May Light and Life-Saving-Scenes the compiler is indebted to Mr. John M. Rogers, printer, of Wilmington, Del.

THE BEACH PATROL.

STATEMENT

Showing the number of casualties to vessels, property involved, property saved, persons on board and lives lost, which have occurred within the scope of the operations of the Life-Saving Service, from and including the Atlantic City Station, coast of New Jersey, to and including the Wallops Beach Station (south side of Chincoteague Inlet), coast of Virginia, for a period of ten fiscal years:

Years.	Number of Casualties.	Property Involved.	Property Saved.	Persons on Board.	Lives Lost.
1885	35	$453,775	$377,775	181	....
1886	46	610,275	516,155	295	....
1887	52	534,795	324,135	320	....
1888	64	1,111,950	830,265	408	5
1889	37	388,045	191,820	187	....
1890	66	909,630	620,835	415	3
1891	37	249,945	207,270	166	1
1892	32	276,655	81,150	214	7
1893	32	724,465	697,985	213	1
1894	46	875,790	747,470	272	....
Aggregate ..	447	$6,135,325	$4,594,860	2,671	17

64

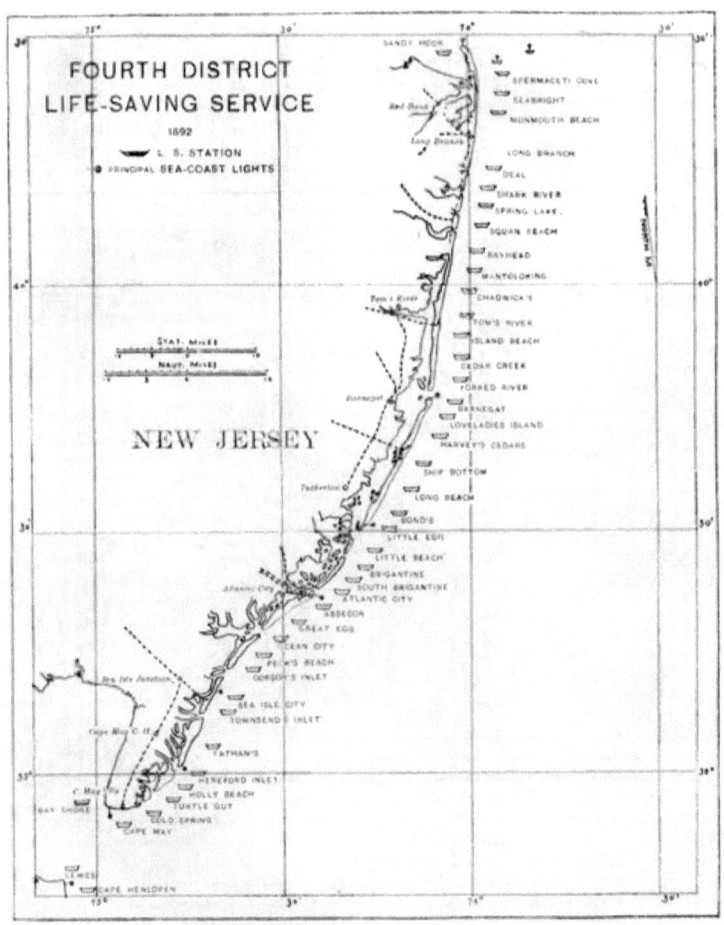

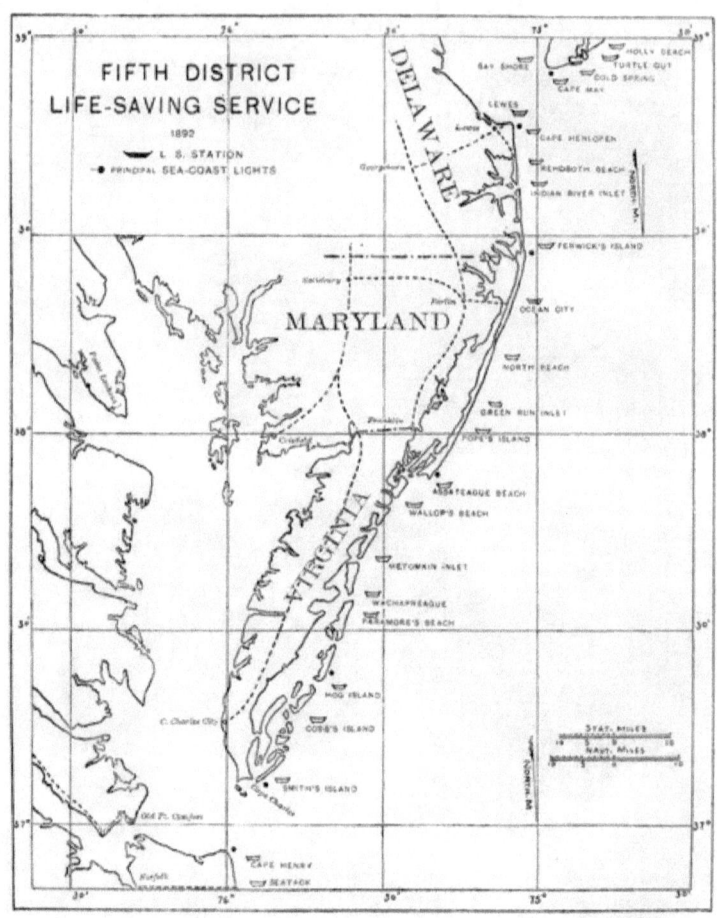

Delaware River Pilot Boats.

PENNSYLVANIA SERVICE.

No. 1—Wm. W. Ker; No. 2—E. C. Knight; No. 3—J. Henry Edmunds; No. 4—John G. Whilldin.

Pennsylvania boats are distinguished by the abbreviation "Pa." upon the foresail.

DELAWARE SERVICE.

No. 1—Henry Cope; No. 2—Thos. F. Bayard; No. 3—Thomas Howard; No. 4—E. W. Tunnell.

City Ice Boats.

The City of Philadelphia owns and operates three Ice Boats (side-wheel steamers) of power and equipment scarcely second to any in the world. Their office is to keep the channels of the Delaware and Schuylkill Rivers navigable in the severest winter weather, and the original intention was that they should be used solely for that purpose; but in time of emergency, when Tow Boats are not at hand and navigation is rendered very difficult, if not impracticable, except in their wake, they accept tows at rates which, though apparently high, pay but a small portion of their operating expenses.

Rates of Towage.

SCALE OF DISTANCES.	Miles. U.S. Survey.	Tons. 70 to 200 and under 70.	Tons. 200 to 500.	Tons. 500 to 800.	Tons. 800 to 1100.	Tons. 1100 to 1300.	Tons. 1300 and upwards.
PHILADELPHIA TO OR FROM		Cents per ton.	Cents per ton.	Cents per ton.	Cents per ton.	Cents per ton.	Cents per ton.
Chester	16¼	18	12	11	10	9	8
Marcus Hook	20	19	13	12	11	10	9
Grubb's Landing	24	20	14	13	12	11	10
Wilmington Creek	28½	22	16	14	13	12	11
New Castle	33½	23	17	16	14	13	12
Delaware City	40	27	19	17	16	15	14
Reedy Island Light-house	46	29	20	19	17	16	15
Morris Liston's (Half Way)	52	31	21	20	18	17	16
Duck Creek Light-house	56½	32	22	21	19	18	17
Bombaby Hook Point	61	34	24	22	20	19	18
Buoy of Middle	71	39	26	25	23	21	20
Ledge Light-boat	77	41	28	26	24	22	21
Buoy on the Fourteen-foot Bank	84	44	30	28	26	23	22
Brandywine Light-boat	90	47	32	30	27	25	23
Buoy on the Brown	94	48	33	32	28	26	25
Breakwater	103	52	36	33	30	28	26
Light-boat on the Five Fathom Bank	128						

A DELAWARE RIVER PILOT BOAT.
[From a Painting by Geo. Essig.]

Lights of the Delaware.

The finest type of light-ship upon the Atlantic coast is the new vessel at Fenwick's Island Shoal, off the Capes of the Delaware. This admirable craft was built at Bay City, Michigan, towed down the great lakes, the St. Lawrence River, and along the tempestuous Northern seas to Edgemoor Station, in the Delaware, where she was fitted out in September, 1892. The

FENWICK ISLAND SHOALS LIGHTSHIP, NO. 52

new vessel is 118 feet 10 inches long, 26½ feet beam, and 14½ feet hold. The principal novelty is the fact that **No. 52** is provided with compound engines, steam whistles, steam windlasses and propeller, thus enabling her crew to not only ease up the strain of her anchor cables, but to take good care of herself in case of going adrift, as did the former light-ship on this shoal in the Winter of '91-2.

FIVE FATHOM BANK LIGHT VESSEL.

CAPE MAY LIGHT-HOUSE.

Another sentinel of the Delaware River is the lonely light-ship at Five Fathom Shoal, a schooner-rigged craft, bearing red hoop-iron day marks at each mast-head, hull straw color, and containing the words "Five Fathom Bank" and "No. 40" upon either quarter. It is located south of east of Cape May Light 18⅜ miles.

Having left this astern, the pilot is guided through the broad space between Capes May and Henlopen, up the bay and river, by forty-eight lights, varying in magnitude from two of the first-class at the Capes to the small lens and tubular lanterns. Eight trumpets and bells warn him in foggy weather. The course of the channel is defined by a series of tangents or ranges. The breadth of the water between the two Capes is 12 statute miles, and the greatest breadth of Delaware Bay is 25 miles. The Bay practically ceases opposite Bombay Hook, where the breadth between the Delaware and New Jersey shores is 4 miles. Below Wilmington the river is 1 mile wide, and, below Philadelphia it has an average width of a half mile.

BRANDYWINE SHOAL LIGHT.

Cape May Light-tower, at Cape May Point, carries a light of the first order, and is 159 feet in height. It is distant 11 miles from Cape Henlopen Light, and 18⅜ miles from Five Fathom Bank Light-vessel. It was established in 1823.

A light is maintained upon each end of Delaware Breakwater, that upon the western end being called the "Front Light."

Upon the seaward side of Cape Henlopen, crowning a high sand hill, is the tower and dwelling of Cape Henlopen Light. The light is of the first order, and is 128 feet above sea level.

In the open reaches of Delaware Bay are Brandywine Shoal Light, Fourteen-foot Bank Light and Cross Ledge Light. Near Bombay Hook is Ship John Shoal Light. Mispillion Creek Light, Mahon River Light, and Duck Creek Lights are upon the Delaware shore. Maurice River Light, Egg Island Point Light,

FOURTEEN-FOOT BANK LIGHT.

and Cohansey Light are upon the New Jersey side of the Bay. The contracted channel above Dan Baker Shoal is indicated by groups of Range Lights.

FRONT LIGHT—BREAKWATER.

SHIP JOHN SHOAL LIGHT.

MARITIME EXCHANGE REPORTING STATION, CAPE HENLOPEN.

CROSS LEDGE LIGHT.

CAPE HENLOPEN LIGHT.

Ship Building.

The Delaware River has long been famous as the center of the ship building industry in America.

The busy era of wooden vessels, when the cheerful sound of the caulking mallet was heard along the water-side, has given place to the age of iron, and Philadelphia has made good use of her peculiar advantages resulting from this evolution. While vessels of oaken material are still made at a number of yards upon both sides of the river, the extensive concerns of William Cramp & Sons, Neafie & Levy, and John Roach & Sons, have devoted their energies chiefly to the production of great commercial and war ships of iron and steel, examples of which are found in a large proportion of our new navy, and in many splendid transatlantic and coastwise carriers of the first class.

The Charles Hillman Ship and Engine Building Company also include iron and steel vessels in the varied work turned out at their large establishment.

In the vast yards of The William Cramp & Sons Ship and Engine Building Company, Philadelphia has the leading plant in the United States.

Founded by a young mechanic, William Cramp, at the age of twenty-three years, in the year 1830, it has developed into an establishment now occupying more than thirty-one acres, and employing an average force of nearly six thousand men.

The number of vessels of all kinds constructed to date is but a few under three hundred, and within the past six months two of the largest

YARDS OF THE WILLIAM CRAMP & SONS SHIP AND ENGINE BUILDING COMPANY.

THE ATLAS DERRICK AT CRAMP & SONS SHIP-YARD.

· NAVAL · VESSELS · BUILT · BY ·
· 1885 · CRAMP · 1894 ·

MINNEAPOLIS. NEW YORK. NEWARK. PHILADELPHIA. VESUVIUS. BALTIMORE. YORKTOWN.

INDIANA. IOWA. BROOKLYN. COLUMBIA. MASSACHUSETTS.

passenger ships in the world, the "St. Louis" and "St. Paul," have been launched with attendant ceremonies of an impressive character, rising to the dignity of national events.

The Atlas Floating Derrick, owned by this concern, is the largest appliance of the kind in the world. The company has gone extensively into the manufacture of ordnance, both for ship and fortress use.

It is believed that the facilities for the further extension of the ship building industry upon the Delaware River, due to the proximity of coal and iron, and the presence of an abundance of skilled labor, are so unrivalled elsewhere, as to secure the perpetuation of the present supremacy in this field of enterprise.

Delaware River Defenses.

The engineers of the Government have perfected an elaborate system of defensive works, upon a scale commensurate with the importance of the ports of the river and the great Navy Yard at League Island, which is to be the central rendezvous and rallying point of our sea fighters of the future.

Fort Mifflin, just below the city, is in the condition which is found at many of the old fashioned defenses of by-gone days, and Fort Delaware has been chiefly valuable as a picturesque accessory of a somewhat monotonous waterscape. This valuable coign of vantage, however, is now in process of rejuvenation.

The site of Fort Delaware was ceded to the Government about one hundred years ago. The present fort was completed in 1850. The island upon which it is placed contains one hundred and twenty-five acres. Fort Delaware is an irregular pentagon, three tiers high, with bastions at the corners. It is armed with nearly or quite one hundred smooth bore 12-inch muzzle-loading cannons, on old-fashioned carriages.

This fort is chiefly famous as a prison camp for Confederates, many thousands having been kept in durance here, pending the great struggle of the Civil war.

The amount appropriated for work upon the fort is $600,000, which is to be expended within five years. The purpose of the Government is said to be to convert it into a modern fort for long-range guns and a torpedo practice station, for which it is admirably adapted.

The Great Navy Yard of the Future.

The site of League Island Navy Yard was purchased by the city of Philadelphia in 1863, out of an appropriation of $430,000, and tendered as a free gift to the United States, and upon December 3, 1868, the Secretary of the Navy, under authority of Congress, formally accepted the property. Up to 1889 the general government had expended only about $1,700,000 upon its League Island property, and it had been used only for limited construction work and repairs to small vessels. For construction purposes it had been

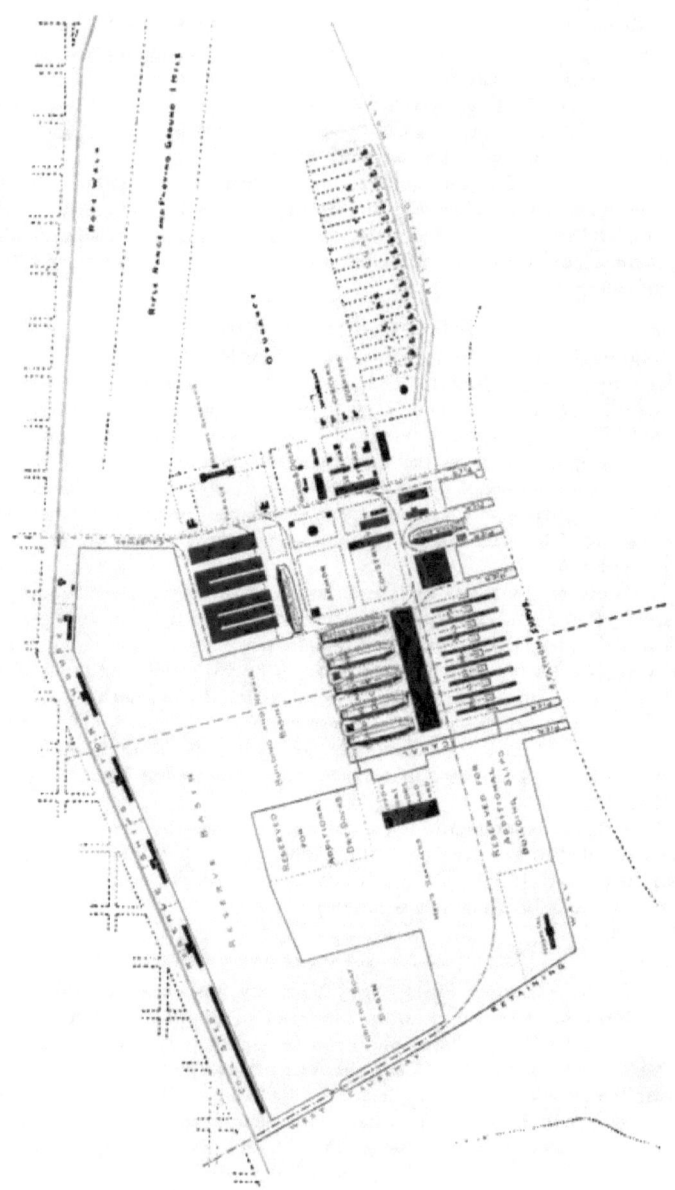

closed from August, 1882. Closely following a report of a naval board (of which the following matter includes the leading features), Congressman A. C. Harmer introduced a bill for the reopening and development of the yard (March, 1890).

The Board of Naval Officers appointed to examine League Island and report plans for its permanent improvement submitted their report to the Secretary of the Navy in October, 1889, and since that time much preliminary work has been done looking toward the great results foreshadowed in their conclusions. The report says, "League Island is situated at the junction of the Delaware and Schuylkill rivers; has an area of 923 acres, which is greater than the combined acreage of the dockyards of Great Britain and any continental power of Europe. The island is formed of alluvial deposits resting upon a bed of gravel. It is separated from the mainland by a sheet of water known as the Back Channel, and connected at the foot of Broad street by a causeway with a short bridge in the centre. It is over 90 miles from the sea, and the rise of tide is usually about 6.2 feet. Salt water never reaches it.

"As a strategic naval point it is, unquestionably, the most important upon the Atlantic coast.

"It is believed that, in the event of hostilities, the ports of the Atlantic coast could be put under contribution by fleets within a few weeks after the declaration of war. Philadelphia alone is the exception, for its position makes it practically impregnable to naval attack, and in addition its blockade would be extremely difficult, if not actually impossible. Now, should League Island be made what the Board proposes it shall be, there will be room in its basins for all the armored vessels we may possess, as well as an indefinite number of cruisers, torpedo, and other vessels of war.

"It is the opinion of the Board that this navy yard should possess all the facilities for building, equipping, and repairing all kinds of naval vessels, including torpedo vessels.

"It is also the opinion of the Board that this is a proper place to establish a plant for the manufacture of great and small guns. It is proposed that the portion of the Back Channel east of the causeway should be filled in and used as a rifle range, and in connection therewith grounds for proving great guns.

"A most important point in connection with this station is the fact that all vessels stored here would depart with clean bottoms, as the water is fresh. The fact of this station being in such close proximity to the coal and iron mines, and in the neighborhood of so many works of different kinds connected with ship building and supplies, is seen in a much stronger light now than when attention was first called to it.

"In this plan it is proposed that ships shall be stored in such a state of readiness that they can be under way within thirty-six hours from the time an order to that effect is received.

"The detailed description of the entire work to be done is as follows:

"1. The conversion of that portion of the Back Channel lying west of Broad street into a deep and spacious reserve basin.

"2. The construction of a smaller but still spacious building and repair basin, opening into the reserve basin and communicating with the Delaware channel in front of the island by a canal.

"3. The location of dry docks and building slips on the space lying between the building and repair basin and the Delaware front, the dry docks opening into the basin and the slips fronting the Delaware, the plate and bending shops being between the two.

"4. The concentration of all the other shops and structures pertaining to ship construction, fitting, repair and armament in the central space enclosed by the building and repair basin, dry docks and building slips on the west, Broad street, the main avenue of the yard, on the east, the Delaware river on the south and the reserve basin on the north.

"5. The utilization of the strip of Government property north of the Back Channel for storehouses for the reserve ships and for coal sheds.

"6. The location of all quarters on the Delaware front of the yard east of Broad street.

"7. The filling in of that portion of the Back Channel lying east of Broad street, and utilizing it for a rifle range and proving ground.

"8. The construction of a permanent retaining wall along the entire Delaware and Schuylkill front of the Government property.

"The capacity of the yard completed upon the above lines will be equal to that of the largest of foreign dockyards, and greater than all of our navy yards combined, owing largely to its compactness, economy and convenience of arrangement and the extent of water front and basin area."

The detailed estimate of the cost of the completed plan thus recommended is $14,565,480.50. The report was promptly endorsed by Captain George B. White, Chief of the Bureau of Yards and Docks, Navy Department, with full concurrence in all of the conclusions reached and the urgent recommendation to Congress to appropriate a sum sufficient to begin the work. The aggregate of the appropriations thus far made for the purpose since the presentation of the report is shown in the following table, and with the rapid increase of our naval list of ships it would seem inevitable that in the early future the yard should and will be put into condition to meet the full requirements of the largest naval demands.

Special appropriations for improvements for United States Navy Yard, League Island, Pa., coming under the cognizance of the Bureau of Yards and Docks, Navy Department:

ACT SEPTEMBER 7, 1888.

For one timber dry dock.................................... $550,000 00
For repairs and improvement of grounds and construction of
    protection wall 75,000 00

Act March 2, 1889.

For landing wharf, Fifteenth street	$26,416 40
For dredging and filling in	75,000 00

Act June 30, 1890.

For rebuilding Broad street wharf	60,000 00
For officers' quarters	10,000 00
For dredging and filling in and paving, etc	25,000 00
For extending permanent sea wall	25,000 00
For construction of light retaining wall	25,000 00

Act March 2, 1891.

For west dry dock pier	87,441 62
For rip rap for protection wall	9,150 00
For continuing light retaining wall	25,000 00
For sewers and flushing tank	5,685 00

Act July 19, 1892.

For extension of protection wall	20,000 00
For light retaining wall	15,000 00
For rip rap, Broad street wharf	6,500 00
For branch sewer	2,100 00

Act March 3, 1893.

For continuation of sea wall	20,000 00
For one pair shear legs	18,000 00
For East dry dock pier	40,000 00

Act July 26, 1894.

For continuation of sea wall	20,000 00
For completion of shear legs	11,900 00
For electric light plant	10,000 00
For completing east dry dock pier	40,000 00

Removal of Obstructions below Philadelphia.

There are six obstructions for large ships between Philadelphia and the open sea—Mifflin Bar, Schooner Ledge, Cherry Island Flats, Bulkhead Bar, Dan Baker Shoal and Duck Creek Flats. The channels over these bars at mean low water range from 20 to 24 feet in depth. They must be increased throughout to 26 feet, according to the Government plan. Unless this be done the great work in progress by the general Government, in improving the Harbor at Philadelphia, will have been in vain. To aid in this vital work, the City of Philadelphia has appropriated $225,000, and, responding to the representations of influential bodies of citizens from Philadelphia, the Pennsylvania Legislature has recently voted $500,000 for the same purpose, realizing the fact that the Delaware River is a great natural outlet for the commerce and products of the whole State. [See Note].

" The freight movements to and from the port of Philadelphia amount to 13,000,000 to 14,000,000 tons per annum, nearly one-half of which consists of the two Keystone State products of coal and petroleum oil. Nearly nine-tenths of the exports from Philadelphia are produced in the State outside of this city."*

---

*Editorial *Public Ledger*.

NOTE.—At the date of this publication, this appropriation has been passed by the Senate, but is still pending in the House.—*Editor*.

OFF THE CAPES.

Harbor and River Improvement.

The plan which is now in progress for the improvement of Philadelphia Harbor proposes the removal of all islands and shoals in the Delaware River between Kaighn's Point on the south, and Fisher's Point on the north —a distance of about six miles—which interfere with a channel about 2,000 feet wide, and of ample depth to meet the future requirements of the port of Philadelphia.

This channel is so located as to permit the widening of Delaware avenue, which fronts directly upon the harbor, from its present width of 50 feet to that of 150 feet, and the extension, from this widened avenue, of wharves from 550 to 700 feet in length. In connection with the extension of these new wharves, it is proposed to revise their previous arrangement, so as to provide docks from 150 to 250 feet in width. The widened Delaware avenue will be provided with a stone bulkhead along its river face, and the necessary railroad tracks connecting with the wharves, leaving ample space for sidewalk and wheelways.

The work of removing the islands and shoals is undertaken by the general Government, while the widening of Delaware avenue and the extension of the wharves will be done by the city of Philadelphia and by private and corporate interests.

The work to be done by the Government involves the removal by dredging of about 22,000,000 cubic yards of material, at an estimated cost of $3,500,000. This work has been in progress two years, and during that time about 9,000,000 cubic yards of material have been removed. Under adequate appropriations this work can be completed in three years.

The plans for the work to be undertaken by the city are well advanced, and at an early date it is anticipated that a number of wharves will be advanced to their new position.

The progress which has been made upon the development of the Harbor of Philadelphia has given an added incentive to the improvement of the river between Philadelphia and the sea, whereby it is anticipated that in the near future a channel 600 feet wide and 32 feet deep, at high water, will be obtained through the few shoal areas, which at present carry a lesser depth.

With the harbor and river improvements realized, the port of Philadelphia will quickly assume her proper place among the leading seaports of the Atlantic coast, with ample facilities to meet all requirements as the entre-port of a large foreign commerce for the whole country.

Delaware Avenue Improvement.

In March of the present year an ordinance was passed by Councils of Philadelphia, placing upon the city plan the outlines of an extension of Delaware Avenue from Fairmount Avenue to Cumberland Street, which

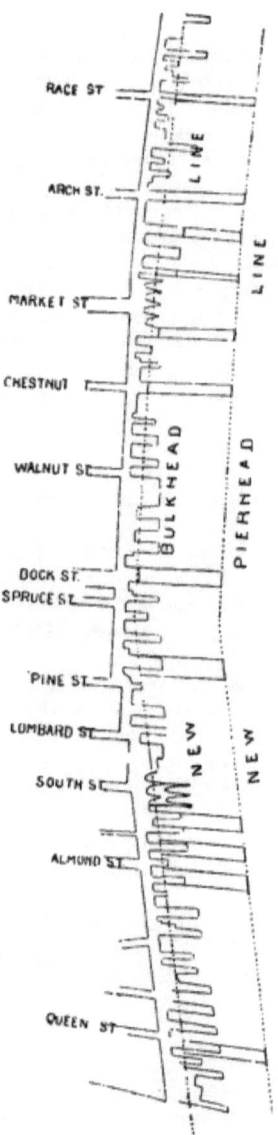

together with the eventual construction of piers to the new Port Warden's Line, permitting the broadening of Delaware Avenue to 150 feet upon the eastern or river side by setting the bulkheads out and its thorough repaving, will result in giving the city a magnificent water front, capable of accommodating the largest ships afloat, and any volume of business which the future may bring to our doors.

The maps produced herewith, obtained by courtesy of the *Public Ledger*, afford an excellent idea of the nature of this forthcoming change. It will be observed that by this plan the present warehouses and buildings now abutting upon the river along Delaware Avenue will remain undisturbed. It is estimated that the entire cost will be about $10,000,000, which will be more than offset in the increased value of properties in the vicinity, leaving out of consideration the incalculable benefits to our trade by sea at home and abroad.

With this great result in view, it is proposed to proceed systematically from year to year, applying such funds as the city may spare in order that the burden may be contemporary with corresponding benefits.

In a message upon the subject sent by Mayor Stuart to Councils, he urged the appropriation of $1,500,000 to commence the work, and to especially permit of the lengthening of the four city piers between Vine and South Streets to the new government line.

There is also available at the present time $600,000, in the hands of the City Trust, being the accumulated interest of a fund willed by Stephen Girard for the improvement of our river front.

Chester, Wilmington and Other Ports.

The principal ports of the River below Philadelphia are: Chester, 14¼ miles; Wilmington, 24¾ miles; New Castle, 29¼ miles, and Delaware City, 34 miles. There are also numerous landings and refuges for small vessels upon either shore, with many small streams navigable for a considerable distance inland, and affording an outlet to market for large areas of highly productive lands and considerable manufacturing industries. Extensive oyster beds are worked at Maurice River Cove, N. J., and in the springtime the shad fishing of the river supplies Philadelphians with an abundance of this fish, which has long been famous for its excellence.

Railroads touch the river at Chester, Wilmington, New Castle, Delaware City, Bombay Hook and Lewes, upon the Pennsylvania and Delaware shore, and at Penn's Grove, Bay Side (opposite Bombay Hook), Port Norris (upon Maurice River), and Cape May, upon the New Jersey shore.

The Delaware River provides an important means of recreation to the masses of the people of Philadelphia. The splendid excursion steamer "Republic" makes highly popular daily excursions from the city to Cape May Point and return. Upon the New Jersey side of the river, a few miles below the city, is Lincoln Park.

The Sanitarium, at Red Bank, N. J., is one of Philadelphia's most noble charities; steamboats especially built for the purpose, a gift to the association by a liberal citizen, carry many thousands of children of the poor classes to this pleasant retreat each summer, where they are provided with food and medical service.

Large industrial concerns are scattered along the Pennsylvania and Delaware shores, enjoying both railroad and wharfage facilities. Notable among these are the Eddystone Print Works, Edge Moor Iron Works, Ship building plant of Messrs. John Roach & Sons, Wellman Steel Works, Penn Steel Casting Co. and Machine Works, Gartside & Sons Mills, Vulcan Iron Works, Chester Pipe and Tube Works, Tidewater Steel Works, and Seaboard Oil Company's plant, all at or near Chester; the Jackson & Sharpe Car Co., Pusey & Jones Ship Building Co., Harlan & Hollingsworth Co., ship and engine builders, at Wilmington, The Delaware Iron Co., at New Castle, Del., and the large plant of the Bear Creek Refining Co., Limited, and the Crescent Oil Co., Limited, at Marcus Hook.

TERMINAL AND WORKS OF THE BEAR CREEK REFINING CO., LIMITED, AND CRESCENT OIL CO., LIMITED AT MARCUS HOOK.

The following information of the magnitude of the oil refining and shipping business conducted at this point may prove interesting.

Marcus Hook, Pa., is the terminal of the Crescent Pipe Line Co. Here are also located the works **of the Bear Creek Refining Co., Limited, and the** Crescent Oil Co., Limited.

THE CRESENT PIPE LINE.—Extending from Gregg Station (McDonald Oil Field), Alleghany County, Pa., to Marcus Hook, Pa., on the Delaware River near **Philadelphia,** one single line of 5 and 6 inch pipe, 265 miles; branch lines, 16.80 miles; total mileage, 281.80.

W. L. MELLON PIPE LINES —Main line of 5 inch pipe extending from Gregg Station (McDonald Oil Field) southwest to Sisterville, Tyler County, W. Va., 86 miles, branches and feeds, 2 inches, 3 inches, and 4 inches; in oil fields **of** Pennsylvania, West Virginia, and Monroe County, Ohio, 201 miles; total, 287 **miles.**

```
Total mileage of pipe lines . . . . . . . . .    568
    Main line—Mellon Line  . . . . . . . .  86
    Main line—Crescent Line . . . . . . . . 265
                                                 ———
                                                 351
PUMP STATIONS:
    Mellon Line  . . . . . . . . . . . . . .  17
    Crescent Line . . . . . . . . . . . . .    7
                                                 ———
                                                  24
TELEGRAPH SYSTEM:
    The Crescent Pipe Line, miles . . .  420
    W. L. Melon Pipe Lines,   "   . . .  205
                                        ——— 625 miles.
Total tankage for storage of oil  . . .  1,318,076 barrels.
Total capacity of pipe lines, 8,000 to 10,000 bbls. per day.
Total number of tank cars in use  . . . . . . . .   200.
Refining capacity . . . . . 6,300,000 gallons per month.
```

Shipments from the oil dock at Marcus Hook, Pa., for the year 1894:

Bear Creek Refining Co., Limited, gallons, 36,494,971
The Cresent Oil Co., Limited, gallons . . 47,281,973.73
                                         ——————— 83,776,944.73

This is equal to 243,103 tons of petroleum.

This required the loading of 66 steamships, 6 ships, 15 barks, 3 schooners, 39 barges.

Schoolship "Saratoga."

One of the most picturesque incidents of harbor life is the periodical departure of the old United States frigate "Saratoga" as schoolship of this port, filled with embryonic young tars ambitious for glory and adventure. To the fortunate youngsters who are enrolled upon the "Saratoga's" school list what boyhood's dreams are realized as they joyfully trip the anchor and sail away to strange seas and foreign ports; and with what delight do they come back to tell their fond relatives and envious home companions of their experiences.

But it is not all fun on board of the "Saratoga," nor, indeed any large part of the time. The object of the Pennsylvania Nautical School is to make practical sailors—men who can be depended upon to help build up our commerce in peace and man our battleships in war time.

The "Saratoga," an old warship of honorable record, was loaned by the Government to the State of Pennsylvania in 1889. She is under the charge of a Board of Directors. The candidates for instruction must be of good character and physique, between sixteen and nineteen years of age, and of parents who are citizens of the State. They are selected for their good records, intelligence and bearing.

The clothing and general "kit" is paid for by the boy. The tuition lasts two years and, together with subsistence, is free. The instructors and navigators are distinguished naval officers.

The "Saratoga" has recently returned from her ninth voyage in her present capacity, having in the period since assignment to this service sailed more than 80,000 miles, two voyages being made annually.

The following is the route of the voyage just concluded: The "Saratoga" left Philadelphia on January 8th. Her first stop was at Bridgetown, in the Barbadoes, a very pretty town of 10,000 inhabitants, garrisoned by British troops. Leaving there on January 29th, a sail of 310 miles to the island of St. Kitts allowed a stop at Basse Terre, a village of 4000 inhabitants, noted for its extensive sugar plantations. The "Saratoga" left St. Kitts February 27th and reached St. Thomas on March 2d, to spend a week. From St. Thomas to Kingston, Jamaica, the last stop of the cruise, is nearly 700 miles, and required a sail of 5 days, arriving on March 14th. Another week was spent at Kingston, when the "Saratoga" sailed for home on March 21st, arriving at the Delaware Breakwater on April 4th. The cruise required 86 days, 43 under sail and 43 in port. In the summer months the cruises include stops at Fayal, in the Azores; Southampton, England; Lisbon, Portugal; Barcelona, Spain; Gibraltar, and Funchal, Madeira; so that it may readily be seen that the boys have abundant opportunity to see many countries and study their people. Seventy-two boys were included in this trip.

The "Saratoga" has the following officers: Commander E. T. Strong, U. S. N., the superintendent, has entire supervision of affairs on board. The executive officer is Lieut. E. M. Hughes, U. S. N., who is also instructor in seamanship, and the other naval officers on board are Lieut. J. F. Luby, instructor in arithmetic; Lieut. W. B. Fletcher, instructor in navigation, and Past Assistant Surgeon V. C. B. Means, instructor in geography, and physician.

Lieutenants Luby and Fletcher are soon to be detached for other service.

Naval Reserves.

The Philadelphia contingent of this organization has its headquarters upon the old U. S. S. "St. Louis," which has been brought up from League Island and moored at Race Street wharf for the purpose. The command is composed of an excellent class of young men and is officered as follows:

R. K. Wright, Jr., Commander; George Breed, Lieutenant-Commander; and ex-officer Courtlandt K. Bolles, Navigator; Bromley Wharton, Paymaster, and John H. W. Rhein, Surgeon.

Distances from Philadelphia to other Ports in the United States, Canada, West Indies and Mexico.

Halifax	735 miles.	Richmond	375	miles.
Boston	501 "	Charleston	597	"
New York	262 "	Savannah	673	"
Cape Henry	246 "	Key West	1096	"
Baltimore	412 "	New Orleans	1669	"
Washington	432 "	Havana	1141	"
Norfolk	279 "	Vera Cruz	1945	"

Value of Exports and Imports at Philadelphia for the past Fifty Years.

Years.	Exports.	Imports.	Years.	Exports.	Imports.
1845	$3,574,363	$8,159,227	1870	$16,694,478	$14,952,371
1846	4,751,005	7,989,396	1871	28,688,551	20,820,374
1847	8,544,391	9,587,516	1872	20,484,803	26,824,333
1848	5,732,333	11,147,584	1873	29,683,186	29,186,925
1849	5,343,421	10,645,500	1874	29,878,911	25,004,785
1850	4,501,606	12,066,154	1875	31,836,727	24,011,014
1851	5,356,039	14,168,751	1876	59,539,450	21,000,000
1852	5,828,571	14,785,917	1877	37,823,356	20,126,032
1853	6,527,996	18,834,410	1878	48,362,116	31,048,197
1854	10,104,416	21,359,306	1879	50,685,838	27,224,549
1855	5,274,338	15,309,935	1880	46,589,584	38,933,832
1856	7,144,488	16,585,685	1881	41,162,957	29,764,278
1857	7,135,256	17,890,369	1882	34,529,459	37,666,489
1858	5,947,241	12,890,369	1883	38,662,434	32,811,045
1859	5,298,095	15,603,769	1884	36,891,605	31,990,309
1860	7,839,286	14,531,352	1885	37,281,739	33,365,242
1861	10,277,938	8,004,161	1886	33,607,386	37,997,005
1862	11,518,970	8,327,976	1887	33,813,024	39,570,687
1863	10,628,968	6,269,530	1888	28,012,879	45,020,132
1864	13,664,862	9,135,685	1889	29,183,468	50,996,802
1865	12,582,162	5,645,755	1890	36,478,554	56,057,013
1866	17,867,716	7,331,261	1891	42,845,724	62,438,219
1867	14,442,398	14,071,765	1892	60,274,024	63,277,781
1868	15,706,445	14,218,365	1893	43,416,955	58,870,186
1869	15,872,249	16,414,535	1894	37,441,000	51,553,704

Commerce of the Port of Philadelphia for the Past Ten Years.

American Vessels entered from Foreign Ports.

Years.	Cargo. Vessels.	Cargo. Tons.	Ballast. Vessels.	Ballast. Tons.
1885	433	210,023	4	3,560
1886	417	127,518	4	1,070
1887	323	169,747	7	9,356
1888	348	187,734	4	1,789
1889	385	223,873	10	13,686
1890	354	210,474	4	3,134
1891	353	221,401	5	4,329
1892	389	263,490	12	12,218
1893	285	211,654	9	7,713
1894	296	245,999	1	85

Foreign Vessels Entered from Foreign Ports.

Years.	Cargo. Vessels.	Cargo. Tons.	Ballast. Vessels.	Ballast. Tons.
1885	743	770,958	107	92,634
1886	862	943,350	59	62,150
1887	1,021	1,091,562	26	31,341
1888	810	829,175	37	42,359
1889	814	884,787	91	117,065
1890	935	1,052,562	136	189,531
1891	844	959,917	172	266,736
1892	914	1,044,240	303	465,305
1893	757	931,558	235	391,624
1894	654	826,798	209	356,669

American Vessels Cleared for Foreign Ports.

Years.	Cargo. Vessels.	Cargo. Tons.	Ballast. Vessels.	Ballast. Tons.
1885	269	153,764	18	6,359
1886	243	143,810	13	4,340
1887	218	148,894	10	3,710
1888	232	137,768	15	4,842
1889	251	178,681	6	2,005
1890	210	144,942	19	7,745
1891	313	224,179	17	7,830
1892	322	243,449	11	6,988
1893	245	210,631	12	4,966
1894	243	235,238	24	19,132

Foreign Vessels Cleared for Foreign Ports.

Years.	Cargo. Vessels.	Cargo. Tons.	Ballast. Vessels.	Ballast. Tons.
1885	763	771,997	25	23,241
1886	695	725,587	32	17,418
1887	762	782,682	65	39,811
1888	611	642,874	104	63,523
1889	615	673,252	82	55,794
1890	772	910,736	104	97,644
1891	677	820,683	95	62,876
1892	946	1,255,259	151	90,069
1893	727	1,018,734	148	95,724
1894	556	892,337	219	134,393

Vessels Arriving Coastwise.

Years.	Steamers.	Ships.	Barks.	Brigs.	Schooners.	Total.
1885	1,633	25	42	20	3,008	4,728
1886	1,610	19	53	25	2,518	4,531
1887	1,539	19	77	52	2,727	4,414
1888	1,517	18	34	22	2,396	3,987
1889	1,443	11	21	8	2,509	3,746
1890	1,376	8	80	19	2,361	3,844
1891	1,474	16	44	8	2,796	4,248
1892	1,472	12	49	5	2,153	4,051
1893	1,471	11	71	7	2,555	4,115
1894	1,444	17	79	10	2,832	4,382

Vessels Sailing Coastwise.

Years.	Steamers.	Ships.	Barks.	Brigs.	Schooners.	Total.
1885	1,707	9	58	48	2,914	4,736
1886	1,841	2	71	50	2,705	4,669
1887	1,819	8	89	69	2,820	4,805
1888	1,597	7	73	49	2,564	4,290
1889	1,647	9	69	29	2,389	4,143
1890	1,563	10	102	37	2,453	4,165
1891	1,684	11	88	27	2,742	4,552
1892	1,551	14	70	30	2,548	4,213
1893	1,554	6	77	15	2,669	4,321
1894	1,564	1	51	74	2,804	4,444

Arrivals at the Delaware Breakwater During 1894.

	Steamers.	Ships.	Barks.	Brigs.	Schooners.	Total.
For orders	42	9	74	20	123	268
For harbor	8	4	18	6	2,333	2,369
In distress	3	—	—	1	1	5
	53	13	92	27	2,457	2,642

Coast Line Distances from Five Fathom Bank (or Delaware Light-ship).

NORTHWARD.
To Northeast End Light-ship. 10½ miles.
To Absecom Light .... 39½ "
To Egg Harbor Light .... 40½ "
To Barnegat Light .... 61½ "
To Highlands Light .... 103½ "
To Sandy Hook Light .... 111½ "
To The Narrows Light .... 123 "

SOUTHWARD.
To Fenwick's Island Light-ship. 33½ miles.
To Winter Quarter Light-ship.. 65½ "
To Chincoteague Light-house .. 74½ "
To Hog Island Light-house .... 116½ "
To Cape Charles Light-house .. 138½ "

NOTE.—The Maritime Rules and Customs of the Port may be had in full from Mr. E. R. Sharwood, Secretary of the Maritime Exchange, Third and Walnut streets, upon application.

United States Coast and Geodetic Survey Charts of the Delaware Bay and River.

No. 124—Delaware Bay Entrance.
" 125—Delaware River, Cross Ledge to Penn's Neck.
" 162—Delaware River, Penn's Neck to Philadelphia, with subsketch,
  126 Bridesburg to Trenton.
" 379—Cape Henlopen and Delaware Breakwater.
" 380—Delaware River, Philadelphia Waterfront.
" 381—Schuylkill River, Philadelphia Waterfront.
" 376—Delaware and Chesapeake Bays.

Shipping Terms.

AD VALOREM—According to value.
AGIO—The premium carried by money above an inferior sort.
BARRATRY—A fraudulent act upon the part of a captain or crew against the interest of a ship's owners.
BILL OF HEALTH—The certificate issued by Consuls and Customs Officers as to health of a port.
BILL OF LADING—A master's acknowledgement as to the receipt of and undertaking as to delivery of a cargo.
BROKERAGE—Commissions charged for securing and transacting business for ships.
CHARTER PARTY—Contract with the owner, agent or master of a vessel for its service.
LETTER OF CREDIT—A letter empowering the bearer to obtain money from the party addressed.
DEBENTURE—Acknowledgement of a debt.
DERELICT—Goods cast away or abandoned on account of wreck or other cause.
DRAWBACK—An allowance by the government under which duties paid are returnable wholly or in part.
EMBARGO—Goverment prohibition against the sailing of a ship from port.
FLOTSAM—Goods floating from a wreck.
INVOICE—A description of goods consigned.
JETSAM—Goods sunk.
JETTISON—To throw overboard goods.
LAY DAYS—Days allowed by charter for discharging or loading a cargo.
MANIFEST—The specification of a cargo furnished by the master of a ship.

Nautical Measures.

Six feet one fathom.
Three nautical miles one league.
Nautical mile, one-sixtieth of a degree of latitude, but defined by the United States Coast Survey as 6,080.27 feet constant length.

Cable's length—one-tenth of a nautical mile, or about 100 fathoms.

A knot, a measure of speed which, as now defined by the United States Coast Survey, is equal to the nautical mile of 6,080.27 feet.

Soundings—upon United States charts the depths are given in fathoms; in open water and in shaded spaces they are indicated in feet.

Directory of Commercial and Maritime Associations of Philadelphia.

THE PHILADELPHIA MARITIME EXCHANGE, Third and Walnut streets. GEORGE E. EARNSHAW, President; E. R. SHARWOOD, Secretary.

PHILADELPHIA BOARD OF TRADE, Drexel Building. FREDERICK FRALEY, President; WM. R. TUCKER, Secretary.

COMMERCIAL EXCHANGE OF PHILADELPHIA, Chamber of Commerce. E. L. ROGERS, President; C. ROSS SMITH, Secretary.

VESSEL OWNERS' AND CAPTAINS' ASSOCIATION, No. 205½ Walnut street. JOHN L. NICHOLSON, President; JAMES F. WALLACE, Secretary.

BOARD OF WARDENS FOR THE PORT OF PHILADELPHIA, Merchants' Exchange. JOEL COOK, President; GEORGE F. SPROULE, Secretary; CHRISTIAN K. ROSS, Master Warden.

TRADES LEAGUE OF PHILADELPHIA, 421 Chestnut street. W. W. FOULKROD, President; J. N. FITZGERALD, Secretary.

GROCERS' AND IMPORTERS' EXCHANGE OF PHILADELPHIA, N. W. Corner Front and Chestnut streets. JOHN W. COOPER, President; JOS. F. HAEGELE, Secretary.

PHILADELPHIA DRUG EXCHANGE, No. 17 South Third street. JOHN LUCAS, President; WM. GULAGER, Secretary.

PHILADELPHIA PRODUCE EXCHANGE. WM. F. EMLEY, President; HOWARD AUSTIN, Secretary.

Public Offices in Philadelphia.

UNITED STATES CUSTOM HOUSE, Chestnut street below Fifth. JOHN R. READ, Collector; J. F. CRILLY, Special Deputy Collector.

UNITED STATES ENGINEERS, Fifteenth and Arch streets. MAJOR C. W. RAYMOND, U. S. A., Officer in Charge.

UNITED STATES LIGHTHOUSE INSPECTOR, FOURTH DISTRICT, Rooms 20 and 30, Fourth Floor, Post Office Building. COMMANDER GEORGE C. REITER, U. S. N., Inspector.

UNITED STATES BRANCH HYDROGRAPHIC OFFICE, Maritime Exchange, Third and Walnut streets. LIEUTENANT-COMMANDER JAMES R. SELFRIDGE, U. S. N., Officer in Charge.

UNITED STATES COAST AND GEODETIC SURVEY, Room 5, Fourth Floor, Post Office Building. R. M. BACHE, Assistant in Charge.

UNITED STATES WEATHER BUREAU, Fourth Floor, Post Office Building. L. M. DEY, Local Forecast Official.

UNITED STATES MARINE HOSPITAL SERVICE, No. 410 Chestnut Street. GEORGE PURVIANCE, M. D., Surgeon in Charge Medical Inspection of Immigrants; G. T. VAUGHAN, M. D., Past Assistant Surgeon in charge Marine Hospital.

UNITED STATES NAVY YARD, League Island. CAPTAIN NORMAN H. FARQUHAR, U. S. N., Commandant; WM. J. MANNING, Commandant's Secretary.

UNITED STATES NAVY PAY OFFICE, Room 21, Post Office Building. HENRY M. DENNISTON, U. S. N., Purchasing and Disbursing Paymaster.

UNITED STATES COMMISSIONER OF IMMIGRATION, Room 4, No. 1224 Chestnut street. JOHN J. S. RODGERS, Commissioner.

HARBOR MASTER OF PHILADELPHIA, Southeast Corner Walnut and Dock streets. JOSEPH H. KLEMMER, Harbor Master; W. G. RUTHERFORD, Chief Deputy.

UNITED STATES SHIPPING COMMISSIONER, No. 500 South Delaware avenue. JAMES J. KING, Commissioner.

POST OFFICE, Ninth and Chestnut streets. WM. WILKINS CARR, Postmaster; JOSEPH C. BOGGS, Assistant Postmaster.

INTERNAL REVENUE, Room 22, Second Floor, Post Office Building. WILLIAM H. DOYLE, Collector; FRANCIS B. BROCKEN, Chief Deputy.

UNITED STATES MINT, Chestnut and Juniper streets. DR. EUGENE TOWNSEND, Superintendent, GENERAL GEORGE R. SNOWDEN, Chief Clerk.

UNITED STATES SUB-TREASURY, Custom House, Chestnut street below Fifth. WILLIAM H. BIGLER, Assistant Treasurer; BARNET EARLEY, Chief Clerk and Cashier.

UNITED STATES NAVAL HOME, Gray's Ferry Road. CAPTAIN J. CRITTENDEN WATSON, U. S. N., Governor; COMMANDER J. M. FORSYTH, U. S. N., Executive Officer.

UNITED STATES NAVAL HOSPITAL, Gray's Ferry Road. DAVID KINDLEBERGER, U. S. N., Medical Director.

CITY BOARD OF HEALTH, Room 610, City Hall. WM. H. FORD, M. D., President; A. A. HIRST, Secretary; JOHN J. MCCAY, Chief Clerk.

STATE QUARANTINE BOARD, 604 Sansom street. R. A. CLEEMAN, M. D., President; BENJ. LEE, M. D., Secretary; THOS. WINSMORE, HENRY M. DUBOIS, ERNEST LA PLACE, M. D.; THEODORE B. STULB, Health Officer; H. C. BOENNING, M. D., Quarantine Physician.

QUARANTINE OFFICE, 604 Sansom street. THEODORE B. STULB, Health Officer. Office Hours: 9 A. M. to 5 P. M. Sundays and Holidays excepted.

Health Certificate to be presented (or, when State Quarantine Service is suspended, affidavit to be made) within twenty-four hours after vessel's arrival at port of entry. Fees to be paid at same time and a receipt or health ticket to be furnished thereupon by the officer in charge.

FEES.

Any Steam Vessel arriving from a foreign port $10 00
" Sailing " " " " " 5 00
" Coasting Vessel, Sail or Steam, arriving from a port South of St. Mary River 2 50

Section 6 of the Act approved June 5, 1893, provides that no fees shall be collected from vessels other than above specified.

Foreign Consuls at Philadelphia.

ARGENTINE REPUBLIC—EDWARD SHIPPEN, No. 532 Walnut street.
AUSTRIA-HUNGARY—ALFRED J. OSTHEIMER, Consul, No. 831 Arch street; ARNOLD KATZ, Vice-Consul, No. 128 Walnut street.
BELGIUM—HENRY PHILLIPS, JR., No. 524 Walnut street.
BRAZIL—JOHN MASON, JR., No. 319 Walnut street.
CHILI—EDWARD SHIPPEN, No. 532 Walnut street.
COREA—DR. R. H. DAVIS, No. 204 Franklin street.
DENMARK—J. N. WALLEM, Vice-Consul, No. 122 South Second street.
ECUADOR—EDWARD SHIPPEN, No. 532 Walnut street.

France—Louis Vossion, No. 524 Walnut street.
German Empire—C. H. Meyer, Consul; Frederick Dalvigne, Vice-Consul, No. 227 Chestnut street.
Great Britain—Robt. Charles Clipperton, Consul; C. Clipperton, Vice-Consul, No 708 Washington square.
Greece—S. Edwin Megargee (Acting), No. 502 Walnut street.
Hawaii—Dr. R. H. Davis, No. 204 Franklin street.
Hayti—Vacant.
Honduras—Solomon Foster, Jr., Pottsville, Pa.
Italy—A. G. Slaviz (Acting), No. 259 S. Fourth street.
Liberia—Thomas J. Hunt, No. 623 Walnut street.
Mexico—Vacant.
Netherlands—Arnold Katz, Vice-Consul, No. 128 Walnut street.
Nicaragua—Henry C. Potter, No. 40 S. Delaware avenue.
Norway—J. N. Wallem, Vice-Consul, No. 122 S. Second street.
Portugal—John Mason, Jr., No. 319 Walnut street.
Russia—S. Edwin Megargee, Acting Vice-Consul, No. 502 Walnut street.
Spain—Jose Congosto, No. 222 S. Third street; Eduardo Fornias, Acting Vice-Consul, No. 711 Pine street.
St. Domingo—Thomas B. Wanamaker, Thirteenth and Market streets.
Sweden—J. N. Wallem, Vice-Consul, No. 122 S. Second street.
Switzerland—Rudolph Koradi, Consul, No. 314 York avenue; Werner Itschner, Vice- Consul, No. 712 Market street.
Turkey—Vacant.
Uraguay—Eduardo Fornias, No. 711 Pine street.
Venezuela—Rufino B. Fombona, No. 952 N. Seventh street.

PHILADELPHIA MARITIME EXCHANGE

1895-1896

During the preparation of this book the following officers and committees have been elected for the terms specified.

Election on April 18, 1895

GEO. E. EARNSHAW, President.
THOMAS WINSMORE, Vice-President.
PHILIP FITZPATRICK, Honorary Vice-President.
J. S. W. HOLTON, Treasurer.
E. R. SHARWOOD, Secretary.
ELISHA CROWELL, Assistant Secretary.
JOHN F. LEWIS, Solicitor.

DIRECTORS

Until April, 1896
SAMUEL T. KERR
J. N. WALLEM
J. S. W. HOLTON
GEO. H. HIGBEE
L. Y. SCHERMERHORN
CHAS. F. GILLER
JOHN H. THOMPSON

Until April, 1897
CHARLES E. MATHER
EDWIN S. CRAMP
F. A. VON BOYNEBURGK
JOSIAH MONROE
JOSEPH A. BALL
GEO. HARRISS, JR.

Until April, 1898
FRANK L. NEALL
THOMAS WINSMORE
GEO. E. EARNSHAW
WM. C. BUTLER
GEO. D. ALI
B. HUMBURG

COMMITTEES

Finance
JOSIAH MONROE
JOHN H. THOMPSON
JOSEPH A. BALL

COMMITTEES (Continued)

Harbor, Pilotage and Station
FRANK L. NEALL
EDWIN S. CRAMP
J. S. W. HOLTON
GEO. H. HIGBEE
CHAS. F. GILLER

Floor and Library
J. S. W. HOLTON
SAMUEL T. KERR
GEO. HARRISS, JR.

Commerce and Transportation
THOMAS WINSMORE
L. Y. SCHERMERHORN
WM. C. BUTLER
GEO. D. ALI
B. HUMBURG

Membership
CHARLES E. MATHER
J. N. WALLEM
F. A. VON BOYNEBURGK

Executive
GEO. E. EARNSHAW
THOMAS WINSMORE
FRANK L. NEALL
J. S. W. HOLTON
CHARLES E. MATHER
JOSIAH MONROE

WM. SELLERS & CO.
(INCORPORATED)
PHILADELPHIA, PA.

MANUFACTURERS OF

MACHINE TOOLS
For Working Iron and Steel

CRANES

Traveling Cranes

Jib Cranes

Dock Cranes, Etc.

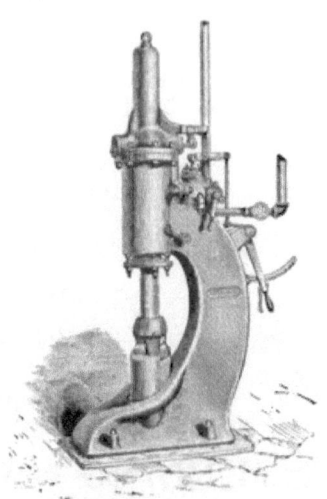

INJECTORS
for Locomotive, Marine and Stationary Boilers

SHAFTING
and all its Appurtenances for Transmitting Power

TURNTABLES
for Locomotives, Cars, Etc.

MECHANICAL STOKERS
for Automatically Feeding Fuel to Boilers

The CHARLES HILLMAN
Ship and Engine Building Company

Machinists, Boiler Makers, Blacksmiths, Pattern Makers, Ship Joiners, Painters, Iron and Brass Founders, and Makers of Propeller Wheels - -

Builders of Iron, Steel and Wood Vessels, Tugs and Yachts, Engines, Boilers, Tanks, &c., &c., &c.

Facilities for Repairing Vessels and Engines with Economy and Dispatch

MARINE RAILWAY

Office and Works, Beach above Palmer Street

PHILADELPHIA, PENNA.

STERLING ⊛ COAL ⊛ COMPANY
POWELTON COALS

GENERAL OFFICES:

419 Walnut Street, Philadelphia, Pa.
29 Broadway, New York.
5 Custom House St., Boston, Mass.

GENERAL EUROPEAN AGENTS:

Hull, Blyth & Co., 1 Fenchurch Ave.,
London, E. C., England.
Cable Address: "Vapor," London.

CABLE ADDRESS:

"*Powelton,*" Philad'a, New York City and Boston.   "*National,*" Baltimore, Md.
"*Dixon,*" Savannah, Ga.

The attention of steamship owners is particularly invited to THESE CELEBRATED COALS as

A FUEL FOR STEAMSHIP SERVICE.

THE POWELTON COALS are comparatively free from sulphur and other impurities, burn freely, and make steam quickly. Their CALORIFIC POWER is very high; economical in consumption; small percentage of ash.

The Analyses of the Powelton Coals have been made by the highest chemical authorities in the United States and England.

THE POWELTON COALS contain fully 95.54 per cent. of steam generating properties, which is most conclusive proof of their desirability as a

STEAM GENERATOR.

Orders received by cable or from captains of steamers will receive most prompt attention.

Kensington Engine Works, Limited
FRANCIS BROS.
Kinyoun-Francis Disinfecting Machinery

BUCKEYE AUTOMATIC ENGINES

KENSINGTON FEED HEATERS

AND SPECIALTIES FOR STEAM AND POWER PLANTS COMPLETE

BEACH and VIENNA STS.
PHILADELPHIA

City Office, 704 Arch St.

SPRECKELS SUGAR REFINING COMPANY

REFINED SUGARS AND SYRUP

REFINERY	OFFICE
Foot of Reed Street	Stock Exchange Place

PHILADELPHIA

PHILADELPHIA CORLISS ENGINES

BUILT BY
PHILADELPHIA ENGINEERING WORKS, LIMITED,
PHILADELPHIA, PA.

CHARLES D. BARNEY & CO.

𝕭𝖆𝖓𝖐𝖊𝖗𝖘 𝖆𝖓𝖉 𝕭𝖗𝖔𝖐𝖊𝖗𝖘

No. 122 South Fourth Street, Philadelphia

Investment Securities. Stocks and Bonds Bought and Sold on Commission and Carried on Favorable Terms

Deposits Received on Interest, Subject to Check at Sight

The Man on the Look=Out
For Hats that wear well and look well, should buy

STETSON HATS

Standards for Quality, Style, Finish and Durability. Ask your Hatter for them and see that "JOHN B. STETSON CO." is stamped on the sweat leather.

JOHN B. STETSON CO.

Retail Department, 1108 Chestnut St.   PHILADELPHIA

Men's Shirts To Order

Skilled cutters and competent finishers employed in a factory fitted with every modern appliance for prompt and accurate work, coupled with the use of only the best qualities of Linens and Muslins, have placed the Shirts we make in the very front rank of excellence.

These are the chief reasons for the marked success of our business in custom-made shirts. They have attained a reputation for fit, workmanship and wearing qualities that is unsurpassed in the shirt-making world.

Prices are the lowest possible for such high-class work.

Self-measurement blanks sent when desired.

Strawbridge & Clothier, Philadelphia

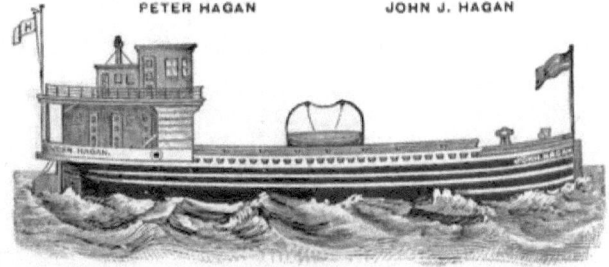

PETER HAGAN & CO.
LIGHTERAGE and TRANSPORTATION
No. 218 Walnut Street

Barges from 100 to 1200 tons for lightering, and steam tugs for towing. Also, tugs with wrecking pumps furnished at short notice. Telephone call, 3309.

BROCKIE & WELSH

WILLIAM BROCKIE
SAMUEL WELSH

Fire and Marine Insurance

DEALERS IN

WHITE OAK AND YELLOW PINE RAILROAD TIES

AND GENERAL SHIPPING AND COMMISSION MERCHANTS

Telephone No. 316   S. E. Cor. 4th and Walnut Sts., Phila.

Philadelphia Shipping Company

Atlantic-Transport—Johnston-Trident Line

Direct Weekly Service between Philadelphia and London and Swansea

Loading and Discharging Piers at Philadelphia and London

PHILADELPHIA—Washington Avenue, Delaware River
LONDON . . .—West India Docks and Victoria Docks

FOR RATES OF FREIGHT AND OTHER INFORMATION APPLY TO

P. F. YOUNG, General Manager

303 WALNUT STREET, PHILADELPHIA

Newport News Shipbuilding and Dry Dock Company
WORKS AT NEWPORT NEWS, VA. (ON HAMPTON ROADS)

Equipped with a Simpson's Basin Dry Dock capable of docking a vessel 600 feet long, drawing 25 feet of water at any stage of the tide. Repairs made promptly and at reasonable rates.

SHIP AND ENGINE BUILDERS

For estimates and further particulars, address

C. B. ORCUTT, President   No. 1 Broadway, New York

Pennsylvania Warehousing and Safe Deposit Co.

CAPITAL ISSUED (Full Paid), $500,000
SURPLUS, ... 500,000
UNDIVIDED PROFITS, . . 200,000

Banking Department, 113 and 115 S. Third St.

Receives money on deposit, subject to check, allowing interest at the rate of TWO per cent. per annum.
Makes cash advances at moderate rates of interest upon every kind of staple merchandise in store or in transit. Markets and negotiates loans on stocks and bonds of corporations, railroads, etc.

Storage Department

Receives merchandise, bonded and free, on storage, in its own United States bonded and free warehouses, and offers wharfage facilities for loading and discharging steamers and sailing vessels of the largest class, together with railroad connections with all lines entering Philadelphia.

GEORGE H. EARLE, Jr., President. RICHARD Y. COOK, Vice-President.
E. B. GRIFFITHS, Treasurer. C. WILLIAM FUNK, Secretary.
CHARLES LONGSTRETH, General Sup't Storage Dep't

DIRECTORS

John H. Catherwood	John M. Shrigley	Charles Longstreth
Richard Y. Cook	Joseph Moore, Jr.	Edgar B. Griffiths
Edward Longstreth	Aaron Fries	George H. Stephenson
George H. Earle, Jr.		

SOUTHWARK FOUNDRY AND MACHINE COMPANY

FOUNDED 1836 PHILADELPHIA, PA.

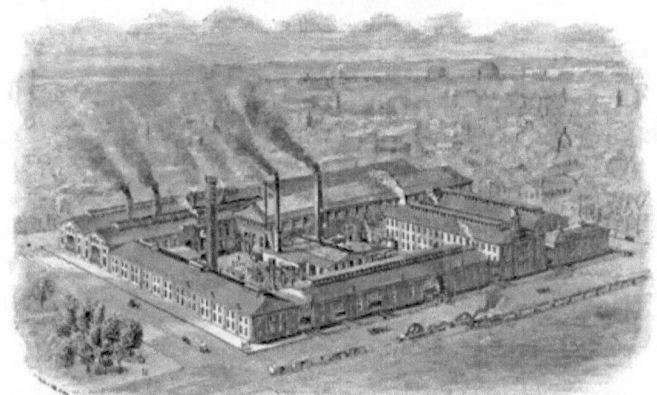

BUILDERS OF SPECIAL AND HEAVY MACHINERY
INCLUDING
STEAM ENGINES, BLOWING ENGINES, PUMPING PLANTS, BOILERS, TANKS, ETC.

Cooperage Stock

Office, 119 Almond Street

PHILADELPHIA

WM. H. HORSTMANN COMPANY
Successor to
HORSTMANN BROTHERS & CO.
Manufacturers of

Flags, Burgees and Signals
OF EVERY DESCRIPTION
International Code Signals, Flags of all Nations, Etc.

5TH AND CHERRY STREETS   **PHILADELPHIA**

ALFRED N. CHANDLER & CO.
HIGH GRADE ELECTRIC RAILWAY BONDS

147 South Fourth Street - - - - - - **Philadelphia**

Quotations and information furnished on low priced dividend earning Electric Railway Stocks that promise a material appreciation in value. An experience of many years affords the advantage of intelligent counsel in the making of investments.
Attention given to the organization and financing of corporations

Palace Steamer REPUBLIC

FOR CAPE MAY

Leaves Race St. Wharf 7.30 A. M., Daily, Returning Early in the Evening

DANCING, THEATRICALS, CONCERTS

DINING ROOMS, CAFES AND REFRESHMENT STANDS

A DELIGHTFUL WAY OF VIEWING THE WATERS OF
THE DELAWARE RIVER AND BAY

$1.00   ROUND TRIP $1.00

The Philadelphia Grain Elevator Company

Office, No. 18 MERCHANTS' EXCHANGE

ELEVATORS	STORAGE CAPACITY	UNLOADING CAPACITY
"PORT RICHMOND" (EXPORT)	1,000,000 BUSHELS	350 CARS PER DAY
"TWENTIETH STREET" (LOCAL)	400,000 BUSHELS	100 CARS PER DAY

THE "WILLIAMS STREET STATION" WITH STORAGE CAPACITY 10,000 TONS, AND FOUR LOADING BERTHS FOR STEAMERS OF LARGEST DRAFT.

Operating via PHILADELPHIA & READING RAILROAD and its connections.

CHAS. M. TAYLOR'S SONS

Nos. 17 and 18 Merchants' Exchange

PHILADELPHIA

Steamship Agents and Ship Brokers

Inward Cargo Piers—NOS. 24 AND 25 NORTH WHARVES.
Outward Cargo Piers—WILLIAMS STREET PIER, PORT RICHMOND.

ESTABLISHED 1821.

ANDREW WHEELER, President.
JONATHAN ROWLAND, Vice-President.
STEPHEN P. M. TASKER, Consulting Engineer.
WM. R. McILVAIN, Treasurer.
H. C. VANSANT, Secretary.

MORRIS, TASKER & CO.

INCORPORATED

Manufacturers of

Boiler Tubes, Oil Well Tubing and Casing

Wrought Iron and Steel Pipe and Fittings

Iron and Steel Electric Light and Street Railway Poles

Special Gun Metal Castings for Power Plants

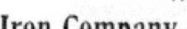

MILLS

Delaware Iron Company
NEW CASTLE, DEL.

Pascal Iron Works
PHILADELPHIA.

CITY OFFICE
224 South Third Street
PHILADELPHIA

x

THE EARN LINE STEAMSHIP COMPANY

S. S. EARNWELL, PIONEER STEAMER OF THE EARN LINE.

THE general office of the Earn Line Steamship Company is at the Southwest Corner of Third and Walnut Streets. The line was established ten years ago by Alfred Earnshaw. In 1887 it became The Earn Line S. S. Co., Limited, and in 1892 was reincorporated under the laws of New Jersey as The Earn Line S. S. Co. The President is Mr. Alfred Earnshaw; and Secretary and Treasurer, Mr. George E. Earnshaw. The latter is President of the Maritime Exchange at this time.

The business of the line is strictly freightage, largely from the ports of Philadelphia and Baltimore to the West Indian ports. The outward cargoes are usually steaming coal. The Clearfield coal is now largely replacing English coal at West Indian points of supply, a movement in which this line has been an important factor. The steamers of the line bring return cargoes of Bessemer ore from Santiago de Cuba, and, in the season, load with sugar from the north-side ports of Cuba, carrying to Boston, Philadelphia and Baltimore refineries.

EARN LINE HOUSE FLAG.

The regular fleet of the line is composed of the

Earnwell, 3,000 tons   Earnford, 3,500 tons
Earndale, 3,500 "   Earnwood, 3,500 "
and Mameluke, 4,000 tons.

The tonnage is reinforced by charter of other vessels, as business may require.

Since the establishment of the line, nearly one thousand voyages have been made by its ships.

The house flag of the line is a white burgee, having a blue border forming the initial "E."

THE ATLANTIC REFINING COMPANY

REFINERS OF

Petroleum and Its Products

FOR EXPORT AND DOMESTIC USE

GENERAL OFFICES
S. E. Corner Chestnut and Fourth Streets

DOMESTIC TRADE DEPARTMENT
125 ARCH STREET

PHILADELPHIA

International Navigation Company's
TRANSATLANTIC LINES

AMERICAN LINE

NEW YORK   SOUTHAMPTON   LONDON

Every Wednesday from Pier 14, North River, New York
No tidal delays. No transfer by tender
Shortest and most convenient route to London. Special trains dispatched on arrival at Southampton
Close connection at Southampton for Havre and Paris, by special fast twin-screw Channel Steamers

PHILADELPHIA—QUEENSTOWN—LIVERPOOL SERVICE

Every Saturday from Pier 54 South Wharves, Philadelphia. Special accommodation for Second Cabin. Steerage at Low Rates

RED STAR LINE

Every Wednesday from Pier 14, North River, New York
Every alternate Wednesday from Pier 55 South Wharves, Philadelphia
Short route to Antwerp, Paris and Continental Points

FOR RATES AND OTHER INFORMATION, APPLY TO

International Navigation Company

305 and 307 WALNUT STREET, PHILADELPHIA

NEW YORK   CHICAGO   SAN FRANCISCO

INSURANCE COMPANY
OF
NORTH AMERICA

No. 232 Walnut Street

FOUNDED A. D. 1792

Fire, Marine and Inland Insurance

ASSETS, JANUARY 1, 1895, $9,562,599.92

CHARTER PERPETUAL

LIABILITIES

Capital Stock..................................	$3,000,000 00
Reserve for Reinsurance.....................	3,858,193 16
Reserve for Losses	372,904 34
All other Liabilities...........................	87,233 32
Surplus over all Liabilities..................	2,244,269 10
	$9,562,599 92
Net Surplus...................................	$2,244,269 10

This Company issues Certificates of Insurance, payable, in case of loss, at the option of the assured, in London, Paris, Antwerp, Bremen, Hamburg or Amsterdam.

CHARLES PLATT, President
WILLIAM A. PLATT, Vice-President
EUGENE L. ELLISON, Second Vice-President
GREVILLE E. FRYER, Secretary and Treasurer
JOHN H. ATWOOD, Assistant Secretary
T. HOUARD WRIGHT, Marine Secretary

DIRECTORS

Charles Platt	Edward S. Buckley	William D. Winsor
Francis R. Cope	Robert M. Lewis	Charles W. Henry
Edward S. Clarke	Edward H. Coates	James May Duane
Clement A. Griscom	John S. Jenks	Henry W. Biddle
William H. Trotter	Edward Hopkinson	G. Assheton Carson
Thomas McKean	Emanuel Straus	C. Hartman Kuhn
John A. Brown	George H. McFadden	

President, THOS. V. COOPER
Treasurer, JARED DARLINGTON
Vice-President, JOHN L. WILSON
Secretary, WM. H. KNORR
General Manager, RICHARD F. LOPER

The Guarantors
Liability-Indemnity-Company of Pennsylvania

Head Office: 713 Chestnut St., Philadelphia

RICHARD F. LOPER, General Manager

Cash Capital, full paid,		$250,000 00
Surplus to Policy-holders,	over	400,000 00
Cash Deposited with State Insurance Commissioners,		261,000 00

Plainest and Most Liberal Contracts Covering

Employers' Liability

Public Liability and Vehicle Risk

Common Carriers' Liability

Workmen's Benefit Insurance

Steam Boiler and Elevator Inspection and Insurance

Machinery Damage and Breakage

Automatic Sprinkler Insurance (loss by water)

The Perfection Blanket Policy of *The Guarantors* combines in one Contract the best features of Liability Insurance.

Full information and rates upon application to

RICHARD F. LOPER,
General Manager

HEAD OFFICE:
No. 713 Chestnut St., Philadelphia

I. M. PARR & SON
(LIMITED)

Grain Merchants

12, Chamber of Commerce

PHILADELPHIA

JAMES L. BRANSON, President   EDWIN R. BRANSON, Sec. and Treas.
BRANSON MACHINE CO.
MANUFACTURERS OF THE IMPROVED "BRANSON"
Knitting Machines
AUTOMATIC RIBBERS
SINGLE OR DOUBLE FEED
SPECIAL MACHINERY TO ORDER

506 St. John Street, Philadelphia

Most of the Illustrations in this Book were made by

THE
Electro Phototype Co.
Engravers by Every Known Method
35 South Sixth Street
F. E. MANNING   PHILADELPHIA

Hoopes & Townsend

PHILADELPHIA

COLD-PUNCHED
SQUARE AND HEXAGON NUTS
CHAMFERED AND TRIMMED, WITH DRILLED HOLES,
WASHERS, SPLIT AND SINGLE KEYS

PUNCHED
CHAIN LINKS

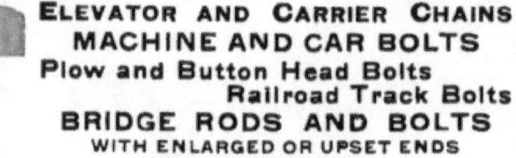

ELEVATOR AND CARRIER CHAINS
MACHINE AND CAR BOLTS
Plow and Button Head Bolts
Railroad Track Bolts
BRIDGE RODS AND BOLTS
WITH ENLARGED OR UPSET ENDS

Boiler Patch Bolts
Wood or Lag Screws
Gimlet-Pointed Coach Screws

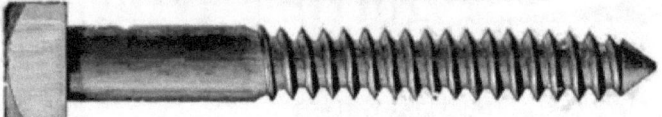

Builders' Iron Work. Pipe and Arm Swivels or Turnbuckles. Straps and Irons for Buildings. Car Irons and Truck Sides. Wharf Spikes.

Iron and Steel

Boiler, Bridge,
Ship, Car, Tank, and
Coopers'

Rivets

J. TAYLOR GAUSE, President
H. T. GAUSE, Vice-President
S. K. SMITH, Treasurer

CABLE ADDRESSES
Rodadura, London
Harlan, Wilmington, Delaware

ESTABLISHED 1836

......THE......
HARLAN & HOLLINGSWORTH
Company

WILMINGTON, DELAWARE, U. S. A.

Ship and Engine Builders

Repairs and Docking Vessels
a Specialty

OFFICE AND WORKS LOCATED ON TIDE WATER AT
WILMINGTON, DELAWARE

London Office, Dashwood House, Old Broad St.
New York Office, Boreel Building, 115 Broadway

THE S. P. WETHERILL COMPANY
FIRST HANDS IN Dry Paints and Minerals
USED IN THE MANUFACTURES AND ARTS
Penn Mutual Life Building, 925 Chestnut St., Philada.
45 CEDAR STREET, NEW YORK

Boiler Maker, Blacksmith, Machinist
Repairs to Iron Ships and Steamboats
Marine Engineering and Boiler Making
Light and Heavy Forgings (under Steam Hammer)
Hoisting Machines for Builders and Contractors
Wood and Iron Tackle Blocks for Builders and Contractors
Hoisting Engines for sale and hire
Steam Pumping Plants for sale and hire
Contractor for all kinds of Iron-Work
Ice Making and Refrigerating Machinery
Filters for Cities, Towns and Dwellings
Repairs promptly attended to
Specifications and Estimates furnished

Builders' Iron Work
All kinds Steam Boilers
All kinds Tanks
Fire Escapes
Steam Engine Builder
Gear Cutting
Friction Pulleys
Steam Yacht Builder
Pattern Making
Pipe Fitting
Contractors' Supplies
Pipes, Coils and Bends.

Cylinders of Steam Engines, Pumps, Compressors, &c., rebored without removing from their present position

JOHN BAIZLEY
IRON WORKS

Telephone No. 1729

Office, 510 S. Delaware Avenue, Philadelphia

WM. O. PENNYPACKER, Jr., President   S. A. PENNYPACKER, Vice-President   GEO. E. BARRETT, Treasurer

Quaker City Cooperage Co.

Manufacturers of **Slack Barrels**

Twenty-Third and Washington Ave.

PHILADELPHIA

FALL RIVER LINE   BETWEEN NEW YORK AND BOSTON

The Fall River Line long since took place among the foremost transportation-systems of the country, and has for many years been recognized as the peer of any of its class by all sorts and conditions of people. The business of this line is continuous throughout the year, all facilities, accommodations, comforts and appliances being equally desirable and perfect in Winter as in Summer. In the course of time these facts have become generally known, until the great majority of the public well understands that at all seasons of the year the steamboats of this line are the same great floating hotels; making safe, rapid, sure and satisfactory trips and unfailing connections throughout every period. Its quintette of steamboats, the **PRISCILLA, PURITAN, PLYMOUTH, PILGRIM** and **PROVIDENCE**, are unequalled in the world elsewhere by similar enterprise; and this vast and restless agency is, indeed, one of the wonders of the century. Music, and all features for the satisfaction or delighting of patrons, are unvarying the whole year round.

FROM NEW YORK—Steamers leave pier 28 (old number), North River, foot of Murray Street, at 5.00 P. M.

FROM BOSTON—Trains connecting with steamers at Fall River (49 miles) leave Park Square Station (N. Y., N. H. & H. R. R.—Old Colony System) at 6.00 P. M.

Sunday trips are omitted during January, February and March.

Tickets by this route are on sale at all of the principal ticket offices in the United States and Canada.

J. R. KENDRICK, President, Boston.   S. A. GARDNER, Superintendent, New York.
    GEO. L. CONNOR, Pass. Traf. Mgr., New Haven.   O. H. TAYLOR, Gen'l Pass. Agt., New York.

O. G. Hempstead & Son

Shipping and Commission Merchants

and STEAMSHIP AGENTS.

Agents of HAMBURG-AMERICAN PACKET CO.

SEMI-MONTHLY SERVICE BETWEEN

PHILADELPHIA and HAMBURG

425 CHESTNUT STREET, PHILADELPHIA

CABLE ADDRESS:—HEMPSTEAD.   Watkins', Scott's and A. B. C. Codes used.

JOHNSON & HIGGINS
Average Adjusters
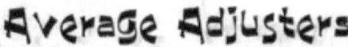
AND Marine Insurance Brokers

NEW YORK, 56 Beaver Street
PHILADELPHIA, 224 Walnut Street
BOSTON, 92 State Street
SAN FRANCISCO, 315 California Street
BALTIMORE, 413 Water Street
NEW ORLEANS, 64 Baronne Street.

Cable Address, "GOURLIE," Philadelphia

J. W. Hampton, Jr., & Co.

Customs Brokers
General Forwarders
Foreign Express Service

41 BROADWAY, NEW YORK
420 LIBRARY ST., PHILADELPHIA

FELTON, SIBLEY & CO.
Manufacturers of **Varnishes and Paints**

136, 138, 140 North Fourth St., Philadelphia

TELEPHONE No. 207   **E. A. HIBBS**   ESTABLISHED 1874

BREAD AND QUARRY STREETS
Above Arch, between Second and Third Sts.
PHILADELPHIA

TANKS
Bath Boilers, Stacks and Heavy Sheet Iron Work

SOMETHING RELIABLE
IF YOU WANT A
HAMMER or HATCHET
Ask For PLUMB'S

ANCHOR BRAND

[TRADE MARK]

Hatchet Always Sharp   **Hammer Will Draw the Smallest Brad**

FAYETTE R. PLUMB, Manufacturer
PHILADELPHIA

GRAHAM-MEYER TORCH AND LIQUID LIGHT CO. (Incorporated)

Manufacturers of
Torches and Liquids for Lights of Various Colors

For Signal Lights and Illuminations of all Kinds. Blue Flash Lights a Specialty

Our Patented Torch is now on the market, and we call the attention of all masters of vessels to its efficiency as a flare-up or flash light. It can be used with Kerosene, Spirits of Turpentine, or any available ignitible fluid. Its superiority over all other kinds of Torches is that it is indestructible; being filled with Asbestos, it will last for years and is ready for use at any moment. It gives a white flame three to five feet high, burns less liquid than any ordinary torch of the same size or larger. The combustion is so perfect that very little smoke is made, and the flame is therefore much brighter. For fishermen's use in signalling, or dressing fish, it has never been equalled, and, we believe, cannot be improved upon. At night you can wig-wag with the Torch and give any signal you wish. **Yachtsmen** will find our Copper Torch of great value in signalling.

Rain or Spray will not extinguish it, and the stronger the wind the better it burns. We have also a

BLUE, GREEN and RED BURNING LIQUID

so as to enable you to make any code of signals you may require.

Office of Corporation, 89 Fulton Street, Boston, Mass.

Philadelphia, 217 Lodge St., John Reese, Agt.   Lewes, Del., R. W. Burbage, Agt.

GEO. M. NEWHALL ENGINEERING CO., Ltd.
136 SOUTH FOURTH ST., PHILADELPHIA

EXAMINATION
OF
BUILDINGS
AND
REPORTS
ON
CARRYING
CAPACITY
OF
FLOORS, Etc.

MECHANICAL
OUTFITS
PURCHASED
FOR
Account of
Clients and
Installed under
Our Supervision

ENGINEERS AND ARCHITECTS
FOR
COMPLETE MANUFACTURING PLANTS
Including BUILDINGS, MACHINERY AND APPARATUS

W. H. SMITHERS & CO.
Builders of the Celebrated ■ : ⁓ ⁞CLAYTON, JEFFERSON CO., N. Y.
THOUSAND ISLANDS ROWING and SAILING SKIFFS

The finest type of pleasure and fishing boat in the world. Suitable for either fresh or salt water.
Also, Square Stern Boats, Yacht Tenders, Fishermen's Dories, Canoes, Batteaus,
Yachts, Steam Launches and Fittings.
Agents for the SINTZ GAS ENGINE, for Launches.

New York Agent, H. C. SQUIRES, 20 Cortlandt Street

Boats shipped, securely packed, to any part of the world. Send for Illustrated Catalogue.

The Clyde Steamship Co.

NEW YORK
5 Bowling Green

PHILADELPHIA
12 So. Delaware Avenue

BETWEEN

New York and Charleston, S. C.	Philadelphia and Charleston, S. C.
" " " Jacksonville, Fla.	" " Jacksonville, Fla.
" " " Wilmington, N. C.	" " Richmond, Va.
" " " Hayti and San Domingo	" " Norfolk, Va.
" " " Turk's Island	" " Washington, D. C. and Alexandria.
" " " Georgetown, S. C.	" " Troy and Albany.

UNSURPASSED PASSENGER SERVICE TO FLORIDA
ONLY DIRECT LINE TO
Jacksonville, Florida, from New York
NEW AND ELEGANT STEAMERS

Through rates of Freight and Passage to all points in Florida and all cities of the South and Southwest. Direct connections with all leading Railroads and Water Lines.

Wm. P. Clyde & Co.
General Agents

5 Bowling Green, New York   ::   12 S. Delaware Ave., Phila.

THE FRANKLIN SUGAR REFINING CO.

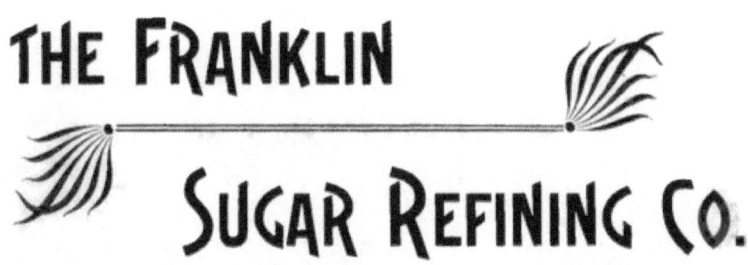

Manufacturers of the Highest Grade

Sugars ....Etc.

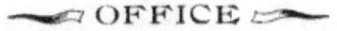

OFFICE

N. E. Cor. Stock Exchange Place and Hudson St.

Refinery: Front and Bainbridge Streets

THE W. J. McCAHAN
SUGAR REFINING CO.

No. 147 S. Front St., Philadelphia

The lofty buildings of the plant in use by the W. J. McCahan Sugar Refining Co. are situated at the foot of Tasker Street, Philadelphia, and form a leading feature in the scene along the river front in the lower portion of the city. The Company has about seven acres of ground with ample water frontage, where two wharves are available for the simultaneous discharge of a number of cargoes. Both the Pennsylvania and Baltimore & Ohio Railroads have terminals here, their cars being loaded at the Refinery doors.

The buildings are the Melter House, Filter House, Pan House, two large Warehouses, Tank House, Boiler House, and extensive sheds. The Company also has a large Molasses House situated about a quarter of a mile distant. Molasses is now imported in bulk by means of tank steamers and pumped directly from the holds to the Tank House, where they have a tank capacity of over 2,000,000 gallons.

The W. J. McCahan Sugar Refining Co. is operated independently of the combination controlling nearly all the similar works in the United States. It is equipped throughout with the most modern appliances for the thorough and economical refining of the raw material into the various high grades demanded by the American trade.

The Officers of the Company are

President, W. J. McCAHAN.   Treasurer, R. S. POMEROY.

Secretary, W. J. McCAHAN, JR.   Manager, JAS. M. McCAHAN.

The offices of the Company are located at Nos. 147 and 149 South Front Street.

American Dredging Co.

236 WALNUT STREET

PHILADELPHIA

FOR THE IMPROVEMENT OF

Philadelphia Harbor

L. Y. SCHERMERHORN,   JAMES N. KNIPE,
      President   Sec. and Treas.

WM. J. BRADLEY,
Gen'l Sup't

RED ✠ STAR ✠ TUGS
PHILADELPHIA

ARGUS	500 Horse Power	JUNO	175 Horse Power
Signal, — · —		Signal, — · · ·	
BATTLER	400 Horse Power	NEW CASTLE	150 Horse Power
Signal, — · —		Signal, — · · —	

⇥ GENERAL DESCRIPTION ⇤

	Length	Br'dth	Engines	Wrecking Pumps	Suct'ns	Suction Hose	Fire Hose	No. of Fire Streams
Argus	120 ft.	22 ft.	20-40 x 28	18 x 12 x 16	2 6 in.	150 ft. 6 in.	300 ft. 2½ in.	8
Battler	120 ft.	22 ft.	20-36 x 28	16 x 10 x 12	1 6 in.	100 ft. 6 in.	300 ft. 2½ in.	6
Juno	85 ft.	18 ft.	15-26 x 20	16 x 10 x 12	1 6 in.	100 ft. 6 in.	300 ft. 2½ in.	6
New Castle	80 ft.	17 ft.	20 x 20	16 x 10 x 12	1 6 in.	50 ft. 6 in.	300 ft. 2½ in.	6

These powerful tow boats are equipped with wrecking and fire apparatus, electric plants, and improved appliances for towing or assisting vessels in distress. Tug Argus has a search light of 6000 candle power (located immediately forward on pilot house) and also two arc lights of 2000 candle power each. By means of waterproof wire the arc lights can be fixed upon any object 1000 feet distant from tug.

The captains of the Red Star Tugs are thoroughly competent pilots, and special attention is given to transporting vessels of deep draught in Schuylkill River, to or from the Point Breeze oil wharves and Girard Point grain elevators.

SEA AND HARBOR TOWING PROMPTLY AND EFFICIENTLY ATTENDED TO

STATIONS—Red Star Dock, foot of Washington Ave., Delaware River ; Point Breeze Oil Wharves, Schuylkill River ; Delaware Breakwater.

PETER WRIGHT & SONS, General Agents, Offices, 307 Walnut Street

C. E. Davis, Jr., Manager   Geo. W. Bellevou, Marine Superintendent

Heat Your House
With a GOOD HOT-AIR FURNACE

The first cost is far less, the management far more easy, and the expense and annoyance of repairs a mere trifle as compared with heating by steam or hot water.

A **GOOD** Hot-Air Furnace is perfectly healthful. There are some that are **NOT** good.

Paragon Furnaces Are Good
WRITE TO THE MANUFACTURERS
ISAAC A. SHEPPARD & CO., 1801 N. Fourth St., Phila.

For their Furnace Book, "HINTS ABOUT HEATING."

FOUNDED 1835

The Delaware Insurance Co.

OF

PHILADELPHIA

S. E. Cor. 3d and Walnut Sts.

CHAMPAGNE OF THE FINEST QUALITY

Lancelot & Co.'s Extra Dry

A Magnificent Rich Wine

M. F. McDONOUGH & CO.

IMPORTERS AND WINE MERCHANTS

223 and 225 South Front Street   Philadelphia

ENOCH MOORE & SONS CO.

Ship Builders and Marine Railway

Foot of Commerce Street

WILMINGTON, DELAWARE

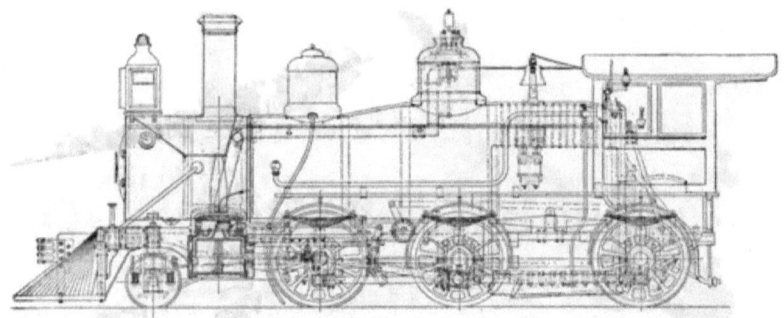

Established 1831 — Annual Capacity, 1,000

BALDWIN LOCOMOTIVE WORKS

SINGLE EXPANSION AND COMPOUND LOCOMOTIVES

Broad and Narrow Gauge Locomotives, Steam Cars and Tramway Locomotives, Mine and Furnace Locomotives, Plantation Locomotives, Compressed Air Locomotives, Oil-Burning Locomotives.

Adapted to every variety of service, and built accurately to gauges and templates after standard designs or to railroad companies' drawings. Like parts of different engines of same class perfectly interchangeable. Electric Locomotives and Electric Car Trucks with Approved Motors.

BURNHAM, WILLIAMS & CO., Philadelphia, Pa., U. S. A.

Berwind-White Coal Mining Co.

Colliery Proprietors
Miners and Shippers of

Eureka Bituminous Coals

Room 305, Betz Building

Broad St. and South Penn Square

PHILADELPHIA

NEW YORK   BOSTON   BALTIMORE

xxx

Gibsonton Mills
ON THE MONONGAHELA RIVER

MOORE & SINNOTT

ESTABLISHED 1837

PROPRIETORS & SUCCESSORS TO

John Gibson's Son & Co.

DISTILLERS OF FINE WHISKEY

OUR DISTILLERY AT GIBSONTON,

On the Monongahela River, with its Extensive Kilns and Malt Houses, gives us unequalled facilities for distilling

PURE MONONGAHELA RYE, WHEAT and MALT

WHISKIES

Of Superior Quality, from Kiln-Dried Grain and Barley Malt

WE HAVE ON HAND

THE LARGEST AND BEST STOCK OF CHOICE OLD WHISKIES IN THE UNITED STATES, all of which are highly improved by age

---

Storage Capacity in Heated Bonded Warehouses, 100,000 Bbls.

PRINCIPAL OFFICE:

232 and 234 South Front Street, PHILADELPHIA

AGENCIES:

NEW YORK,	BOSTON,	NEW ORLEANS,	SAN FRANCISCO,
60 Broad St.	160 State St.	102 Poydras St.	314 Sacramento St.

SAVANNAH, GA.

RAILROAD BRIDGES AND TRESTLE WORK   MILL AND FACTORY BUILDINGS

LOUIS P. EVANS
Successor to COFRODE & EVANS

Engineer and Contractor

S. E. Corner Fourth and Walnut Streets

PHILADELPHIA, PA.

PILE AND WHARF WORK   WAREHOUSES

LESLEY & TRINKLE
Successors to J. CAMPBELL HARRIS & CO.

Portland and Rosendale Cements
PLASTER AND BUILDING MATERIAL

FAIRMOUNT AVENUE WHARF

PHILADELPHIA

W. E. GARRETT & SONS

Scotch Snuff Manufacturers

224 South Front Street

PHILADELPHIA

CHAS. W. PUSEY, President
THOMAS H. SAVERY, Vice-Prest.

WILLIAM W. PUSEY, Treasurer
SAM'L C. BIDDLE, Secretary

Long Distance Telephone, No. 111
Cable Address, "Pusey, Wilmington"

The Pusey & Jones Company

BUILDERS OF

Iron Vessels, Steam Engines and Boilers...

Machinery for Paper and Sugar Mills...

And Heavy Machinery Generally

Established 1848

WILMINGTON, DELAWARE, U. S. A.

Delaware Breakwater
and Lewes, Delaware
Reporting and Telegraph Stations
OF
The Philadelphia Maritime Exchange

For the convenience of Consignees of Vessels and Cargoes using the Delaware Breakwater as a Port of Call, a **Prompt and Confidential Delivery Service** is maintained by The Philadelphia Maritime Exchange from its Station on the Delaware Breakwater as well as from its Branch Office at Lewes, Delaware. All Letters, Telegrams and Cables should be addressed "In care Maritime Exchange, Lewes, Del.," whence a direct wire runs to the Delaware Breakwater.

The Station on the Delaware Breakwater is open day and night for the signalling and reporting of vessels, and experienced boatmen are always in attendance, thereby avoiding unnecessary delay. In order to do away with the **miscellaneous charges**, to vessels in various forms not usually noted at first sight, the Exchange has adopted the following tariff of delivery charges:

TO VESSELS ANCHORED IN HARBOR TO EASTWARD OF ICE BREAKER,		$1 00
" " " WESTWARD	"	2 00
" " OUTSIDE OF BREAKWATER AND	"	3 00

Masters of vessels are invited to make use of the Breakwater Station, and of the Branch office of the Exchange at Lewes, Delaware, which are kept supplied with the Daily Newspapers, Records of Shipping, Port Charges, Hydrographic and Weather Bulletins, etc., etc.

The Cautionary and Storm Signals of the United States Weather Bureau are displayed from the Breakwater Station.

Special Telegrams, announcing the arrival or the passing in or out of any particular vessel, will be sent from the Breakwater Station to any person desiring the same upon application, the charge for which service being **One Dollar**, exclusive of telegraph and cable tolls.

NOTE:—Cable orders for vessels in Harbor or to arrive, should be addressed "**Delbreak**," Lewes, Delaware.

PERCIVAL ROBERTS, President
PERCIVAL ROBERTS, JR., Vice-President

P. W. ROBERTS, Treasurer
FREDERICK SNARE, Secretary

PENCOYD IRON WORKS

Works
PENCOYD, PA.

Office
261 S. Fourth Street
PHILADELPHIA, PA.

Manufacturers of

OPEN-HEARTH STEEL BARS
AND STRUCTURAL SHAPES
CAR AND ENGINE AXLES

Designers and Builders of

BRIDGES   VIADUCTS
TRAIN SHEDS
ELEVATED RAILROADS AND
ALL STEEL STRUCTURES

A. & P. ROBERTS
COMPANY

Andrew Bolger
Teamster and Rigger

Heavy and Light Hauling
OF EVERY DESCRIPTION

13 South Fourth Street

Telephone 126   Philadelphia

Geo. S. Harris & Sons
718-724 Arch Street

Philadelphia, Pa.

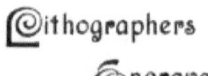
Lithographers
Engravers

General Job Printers

Advertising Novelties
A SPECIALTY

PHILADELPHIA
NEW YORK
CHICAGO

SAN FRANCISCO
BOSTON
CINCINNATI

The...BARTRAM

...A First-class Apartment House

Will OPEN September 1, 1895
For Inspection June 15

LOCATION .... At the intersection of Chestnut Street, Woodland Avenue and Thirty-third Street.
One square from Drexel Institute and the New Franklin Athletic Field.
Within five minutes' walk of Schools and Churches of all denominations.

TRANSIT FACILITIES .... Afforded by this location consist of two-track trolley line on Chestnut Street.
Double line on Woodland Avenue, with a terminus at Chester.
Thirty-third Street direct to Fairmount Park, trolley road in operation.
Market Street cable within one square.
South Street Station, P. R. R., five minutes.
Poweltown Avenue Station, Main Line, seven minutes.

MEALS .... Will be served table-d'hote, the excellence of which will be assured by the service of an experienced chef and a perfectly equipped cuisine.
Arrangements may also be made for private dinners or entertainments of any kind.

CONVENIENCES ... Our own plant for steam heat and electric lights.
Good elevator service.
Bell Boys and janitor for legitimate house service.

TELEPHONES .. Connecting all suites with main office.

OBSERVATORY On roof for use of guests.

For details, address **Russell Hawkins**
General Manager

xxxv

UPPER DELAWARE RIVER TRANSPORTATION CO.

Steamers COLUMBIA, JOHN A. WARNER, TWILIGHT and TRENTON

Leave Chestnut Street Wharf, PHILADELPHIA, daily for Bristol, stopping at Bridesburg, Tacony, Riverton, Torresdale, Beverly and Burlington, connecting at Bristol with the new steel steamer "TRENTON," for Trenton, N. J.; a most delightful excursion to the head of navigation and return. Summer schedule in effect June 1st to September 15th. See times of leaving in Philadelphia papers. A full orchestra accompanies the steamer "COLUMBIA" daily on her 2 p. m. trip. Excursion to Bristol, 40 cts.; Trenton, 50 cts.

Member of American Warehousemen's Association. Established 1855.

Godley's Storage Warehouses

Bonded and Free Storage

Negotiable Receipts Issued

Telephone 3246

Granite Street—U. S. Bonded Stores
Argyle Stores
Queen Street Stores

Philip Godley, Proprietor

Office, Cor. Dock and Granite Sts.   PHILADELPHIA

KEEN, SUTTERLE CO.

PHILADELPHIA   NEW YORK   BOSTON
417-427 N. 3d St.   86 Gold St.   237 Congress St.

IMPORTERS, EXPORTERS, COMMISSIONERS

WILL EXECUTE ORDERS FOR

COTTON GOODS, PETROLEUM, COTTON SEED OIL, OILS, FLOUR, GRAIN, PROVISIONS, LUMBER, STORES, MACHINERY, ROLLING STOCK, RAILWAY SUPPLIES, ETC.

Will make firm offers for cargo and part cargo to all parts of the world. Will purchase and sell on commission in any part of the world. Advances made on consignment. Correspondence solicited . . . .

Highest London and New York References

CABLE ADDRESS
Coatkeen   Members N. Y. Produce Exchange

BRANCH HOUSES AND AGENTS

Europe
London   Manchester   Bradford   Dublin   Paris   Marseilles
Hamburg   Amsterdam   Moscow   Batoum   Madrid
Palermo   Barcelona   Seville   Milan   Florence   Genoa
Ancona   Trieste   Constantinople   Salonica   Smyrna

South America
Buenos Ayres   Pieura   Pernambuco   Mossoro

North Africa
Tangier   Rabat   Oran   Mazagan   Mogadore
Casablanca   Saffi   Tripoli   Algiers

South Africa
Cape Town   Port Elizabeth   King Williams Town   Durban

British India
Calcutta   Bombay   Madras

Arabia
Aden   Hodeidah   Jeddah   Gunfittah

West Indies
Kingston   Port au Prince   St. Thomas   etc., etc.

WILMINGTON & NORTHERN RAILROAD

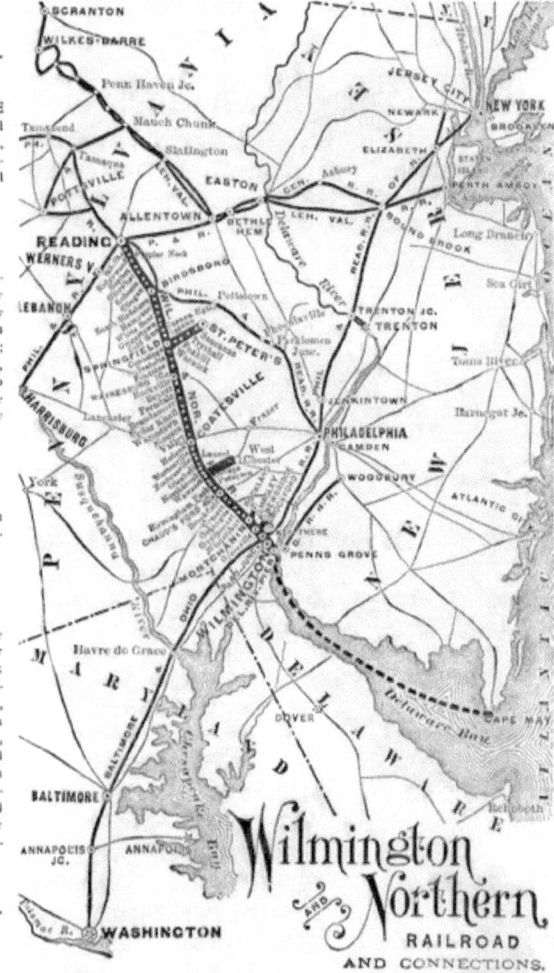

Direct SHORT LINE between Wilmington and West Chester, Coatesville, Birdsboro, Reading, Interior Pennsylvania and New York State.

∴

Direct track connection by float with Edge Moor Bridge Works, Edge Moor, Del.; Delaware Iron Co., Newcastle, Delaware; Delaware River Railroad, Pennsgrove, N. J. Also to all points on Delaware River and tributaries by float or barge.

∴

Tidewater terminus on Delaware River at Delaware River pier.

∴

Through freight service to all points in Interior Pennsylvania, New York State, New England, Canada, the West, Northwest, South and Southwest, via Philadelphia & Reading, Baltimore & Ohio, Central of New Jersey, Lehigh Valley, Delaware, Lackawanna & Western, Fall Brook, West Shore, New York Central and connecting railroads.

A. G. McCAUSLAND, Superintendent
WILMINGTON, DEL.

BOWNESS BRIGGS, General Freight Agent
WILMINGTON, DEL.

Carnahan & Ennis

N. E. Cor. 10th and Walnut Sts.
PHILADELPHIA

Latest English Novelties
in Suitings and Trouserings
always on hand

ENGLISH RIDING TROUSERS, BREECHES AND LEGGINGS A SPECIALTY. LIVERIES OF EVERY DESCRIPTION MADE TO ORDER AT REASONABLE PRICES.

Tailors

GEORGE H. JARDEN,
PRESIDENT & TREASURER

EUGENE Z. KIENZLÉ,
SECRETARY

The Hannis Distilling Co.
Fine Whiskies

218 South Front St., and 143 Dock St., Philadelphia

DISTILLERIES

Hannisville, Martinsburg, West Virginia   Mount Vernon, Baltimore, Maryland

---

Legitimate Detective Work in all its Branches
at Reasonable Rates

KEYSTONE DETECTIVE AGENCY

No. 532 WALNUT STREET
PHILADELPHIA, PA.

C. HALYBURTON, JR.,   217 Walnut St., Philadelphia

STEAMSHIP AND ENGINEER SUPPLIES

Ship Chandlery   High Grade Oils *for the Marine Trade*

JOS. E. GILLINGHAM   DAVID H. GARRISON   GEO. WARNER   COURTLAND Y. WHITE

GILLINGHAM, GARRISON & CO., Limited

Steam Saw Mills, Lumber Yard & Planing Mills

Oregon Pine, Yellow Pine, White Pine, Ship Timber and Decking

943 RICHMOND STREET, PHILADELPHIA

THE ROBERT HARE POWEL CO.

MINERS AND SHIPPERS OF

EL MORA SEMI-BITUMINOUS COALS

421 Chestnut Street, Philadelphia

W. F. HAGAR J. H. THOMPSON

W. F. HAGAR & CO.

Ship Brokers and Commission Merchants

N. E. Cor. Walnut and 3d Sts., Philadelphia

Agents New Bedford Copper Co.

CABLE ADDRESS, "HAGAR" USE "WATKINS CODE"

WILLIAMSON & CASSEDY
RAILWAY AND STEAMSHIP SUPPLIES

526 MARKET STREET PHILADELPHIA, PA.

EVERY DESCRIPTION OF **Fireworks** For Marine Purposes

Government Contractors, also to the principal Steamship Companies and Yacht Clubs of the world.

MANUFACTURED BY **PAIN'S FIREWORKS CO.**

SOLE PYROTECHNISTS AT MANHATTAN BEACH AND AT WORLD'S FAIR, CHICAGO

102 WILLIAMS ST., NEW YORK

Price Lists and Catalogues on application AND AT LONDON AND LIVERPOOL

BROWN BROTHERS & CO.

S. E. Cor. 4th and Chestnut Sts., Philadelphia

59 Wall Street, New York   ALEX. BROWN & SONS
50 State Street, Boston   Baltimore and Calvert Sts., Baltimore

Members of the Stock Exchanges of New York, Philadelphia and Baltimore

Buy and Sell Bonds and Stocks on Commission

    First-Class Investment Securities a Specialty

        Money Received on Deposit and Interest Allowed

Buy and Sell Bills of Exchange
And Cable Transfers of Money

On Great Britain and Ireland, France, Germany, Belgium, Holland, Switzerland, Norway, Denmark, Sweden and Australia.

Issue Commercial and Travelers' Credits

In Sterling, available in any part of the world. In Francs, for use in Martinique and Guadaloupe; and in Dollars, for use in this country, Canada, Mexico, the West Indies and South America.

Make Collections of Drafts

Drawn abroad on all points in the United States and Canada, and of Drafts drawn in the United States on foreign countries.

Their London House, Messrs. BROWN, SHIPLEY & CO., receive accounts of American banks, firms and individuals, upon favorable terms

S. & JAS. M. FLANAGAN

REAL ESTATE...
      STEAMBOATS....
STEAM TUGS....
      STEAM PUMPS...

With Wrecking and Submarine appurtenances.

226 Walnut Street, Philadelphia

Londonderry...

LITHIA SPRING WATER

STILL and SPARKLING

...FOR
Rheumatism, Dyspepsia, Gout, Gravel, Malaria, Brights and all Kidney Diseases . . . . .

THE BEST TABLE WATER
In the Market to-day.

ALL DEALERS, OR

Shinn & Company

...PHILADELPHIA, PA.

Works of the J. G. BRILL COMPANY

Builders of Railway, Cable and Electric Cars

ELECTRIC MOTOR TRUCKS AND CABLE GRIP TRUCKS

PHILADELPHIA

Girard Point Storage Company

PHILADELPHIA

EXPORT GRAIN ELEVATORS

Elevator A, Girard Point, Capacity - - 800,000 bushels.
Elevator B, Girard Point,   "   - - 1,250,000   "
Elevator C, Washington Ave., "   - -   450,000   "

GIRARD POINT

Situated at one of the principal termini of the

PENNSYLVANIA RAILROAD

Has ample dock facilities for the largest class of ocean vessels.

Storage for Merchandise Cargoes and Iron Ore.

Two Ore Vessels expeditiously discharged at one time, directly into railroad cars.

C. B. ROWLEY, Manager

Room 200   305 Walnut Street

HENRY LEVIS & CO.

Iron and Steel

New Steel Rails, Splice Bars, Spikes
Old Rails, Scrap Iron, Etc.

26 South Fifteenth Street

PHILADELPHIA, PA.

MARINE INSURANCE

British and Foreign Marine Insurance Co., Ltd.

LIVERPOOL

ASSETS, - $7,750,000

MATHER & CO., Attorneys

229 and 231 Walnut Street

PHILADELPHIA

FRANK SAMUEL

Ores—Iron and Manganiferous

STEEL, SCRAP AND FINISHED MATERIAL

IRON

OF ALL CHARACTER

Export Trade a Specialty   Cable Address, "Samrak"

PHILADELPHIA, PA.

O. S. JANNEY & CO.

IMPORTERS OF

INDIGO, CUTCH, GAMBIER, SICILY SUMAC, &c.

AND DEALERS IN

DYESTUFFS, EXTRACTS and CHEMICALS

70 KILBY STREET	**8 and 10 LETITIA STREET**
BOSTON	PHILADELPHIA

EXCLUSIVE DESIGNS IN Fine Furniture, Draperies and Interior Decorations

THE HALE & KILBURN MFG. CO.
48 and 50 North Sixth Street, Philadelphia

Makers of Improved **FOLDING BED** of Unique Designs

Commercial Furniture and Fixtures

We Want the Delaware River Deepened

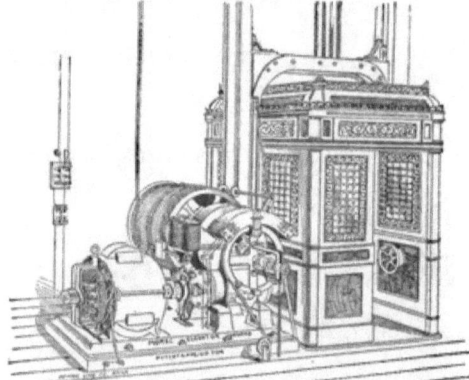

SO WE CAN SEND OUR

PASSENGER and FREIGHT

ELEVATORS

to all parts of the world in ships sailing from this port, instead of sending them from New York as we are compelled to do now.

MORSE, WILLIAMS & Co.
Works: Frankford Ave., Wildey and Shackamaxon Sts.
PHILADELPHIA

CREW·LEVICK·CO.

·PRODUCERS·
REFINERS AND EXPORTERS OF
·PETROLEUM·PRODUCTS·
·PHILADELPHIA·

BRANCH OFFICES
NEW YORK
CHICAGO
SAVANNAH
BALTIMORE
SAN FRANCISCO
LONDON
LIVERPOOL
HAMBURG
ANTWERP
PARIS

Refineries,
SOUTH CHESTER, PA.
WARREN, PA.

www.ingramcontent.com/pod-product-compliance
Lightning Source LLC
Chambersburg PA
CBHW030346170426
43202CB00010B/1269